World Register of University Studies of Jewish Civilization

Inventory of Holdings-Number I

International Center for University Teaching of Jewish Civilization

Academic Chairman: Moshe Davis

Director: Natan Lerner

World Register of University Studies in Jewish Civilization

Director: Mervin F. Verbit

Coordinator: Florinda Goldberg

Regional Associates: Doris Bensimon, France

Naomi Cohen, USA

Michael Rubin, Canada

The following people also gave significant assistance in gathering
material in the countries indicated:

Marcus Arkin (South Africa); Edy Kaufman (USA); William Orbach (USA);
Alvin Rosenfeld (USA); Geula Solomon (Australia)

Inquiries and additional information can be sent to the World Register
at:

P.O.B. 4234
Jerusalem 91042
Israel
Telephone: 02-633005, 699032

World Register of University Studies of Jewish Civilization

Inventory of Holdings-Number I

Edited by Mervin F. Verbit

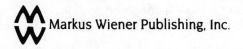

Markus Wiener Publishing, Inc.

ISBN 0-910129-30-4
Library of Congress Card Number: 85-040514

Printed in the United States of America

TABLE OF CONTENTS

I. List of Institutions with Courses in Jewish Civilization (cont'd)

II. Thematic Index (cont'd)

We gratefully acknowledge the assistance of the Joint Program for Jewish Education (State of Israel Ministry of Education and Culture – The Jewish Agency for Israel – World Zionist Organization) and of the Memorial Foundation for Jewish Culture in supporting the overall program of the International Center, and of the Scheuer Foundation for contributing to the development of the World Register.

INTRODUCTION

The International Center for University Teaching of Jewish Civilization was established under the auspices of the office of the President of Israel in 1981 to enrich the teaching of Jewish Civilization in institutions of higher learning around the world. During the last few decades Jewish Civilization has acquired a growing place in university offerings, but that place is uneven in content, style, and structure. As is the case with any vast field, Jewish Civilization can be organized for presentation in various ways. Moreover, since the field is multi-disciplinary, it is found in several academic departments. In some institutions, courses on Jewish Civilization are gathered together in a separate administrative unit; in others, they are spread among a number of departments. Jewish Civilization can be taught as a separate subject, and it should also be--and is--included as part of many larger subjects. As a result of all this diversity, Jewish Civilization is taught in a sometimes bewildering array of courses and course units. Whatever its structure, however, all good teaching requires appropriate conceptual frameworks, significant comparative approaches, and intellectually sound and heuristically effective instructional material.

The International Center for University Teaching of Jewish Civilization operates in its initial stages through several projects whose purposes are to identify the needs of the field and to set in motion activities to meet those needs. Each project is directed and advised by leading professors and is designed to address issues in its area of specific concern. These projects now include:

1

Continuing Workshops in (1) **Modern Hebrew**, (2) **Jewish History: Sephardic and Oriental Jewry**, (3) **Contemporary Jewish Civilization and** (4) **Jewish Political Tradition.** The workshops function through correspondence and annual meetings. They have identified the ways in which the teaching of their respective subjects can be strengthened and are preparing instructional materials that have already begun to find their way into university curricula.

Jewish Civilization University Series (Binah). Much of the important research in Jewish Civilization is published in Hebrew in scholarly journals. In order to make this material available for use in undergraduate classes conducted in other languages, selected articles are translated and adapted for student use.

Training Program for Post-Graduate Students and Junior Faculty. Several promising young scholars from various countries are appointed each year to fellowships which enable them to spend time in Israel studying with senior colleagues in their respective fields and preparing materials which will extend the scope and enhance the effectiveness of their teaching.

Distinguished Scholars Program. Each year a senior scholar is invited to Jerusalem to work on the development of teaching material in his/her special field. The Irving and Bertha Newman Distinguished Scholars of the International Center now include Haim Zafrani of the University of Paris, Sol Encel of the University of New South Wales, and Emil Fackenheim of the University of Toronto.

Teaching with the Aid of Multi-Media Technology. Conventional printed works are increasingly being supplemented in university courses by audio-visual material that can provide an important additional dimension to teaching. Video-cassettes in the field of recent Jewish History are being contemplated in order to convey the kind of understanding that is not fully transmitted through the printed word.

Curriculum Projects are now being carried out in (1) The American Jewish Experience and (2) Jewish History and Culture in the Medieval Period. Other projects are being contemplated. These projects, conducted in the United States, are in coordination with the Hebrew Union College-Jewish Institute of Religion, The Jewish Theological Seminary of America, Yeshiva University, and Brandeis University. They will produce comprehensive syllabi as well as readers for use in university courses in English-speaking countries.

Jewish Studies at Church-Affiliated Institutions of Higher Learning. These institutions have special needs, of course, and this project works with them to enrich their offerings in the various aspects of Jewish Civilization which are part of their curricula.

Jewish Civilization Studies in Universities in Spanish- and Portuguese-Speaking Countries. The specific environmental characteristics of these countries led to the development of a special project. Its goals are to assist in the creation of local committees for encouraging Jewish Civilization studies, to help train university instructors, to provide model programs for courses, and to aid in the development of curricula and textual material. A pilot project inaugurated by the Center at the Universidad Iberoamericana in Mexico City has been operating successfully since 1982.

World Register of University Studies in Jewish Civilization and Resource Library. In order to gather together material on the teaching of Jewish Civilization in one place, the International Center has established its World Register, which includes listings of programs, courses and faculty, as well as a collection of syllabi used in the teaching of Jewish Civilization. The World Register enables people concerned with the teaching of Jewish Civilization to have the relevant facts readily available. It also serves as a resource for those planning courses and programs in the field.

The present volume is an Inventory of the World Register's holdings as of January 1, 1985. In the first section, we list the institutions for which we have information concerning the way in which Jewish Civilization is taught, together with a coded indication of the nature of the material. In some cases, we have full information about courses, programs, requirements, administrative structure and faculty. In some cases we have only partial information. Omitted from the list are Jewish seminaries and teacher training colleges, in which virtually the entire curriculum is, of course, in Jewish Civilization, as well as Israeli institutions.

Needless to say, the collection of truly comprehensive data on the teaching of Jewish Civilization is a vast undertaking. During the first stage in the development of the World Register, material was collected where it was readily available through the assistance of colleagues who were involved in the Center's various projects. The World Register is now moving toward more systematic methods of gathering information, and it is hoped that before long mechanisms will be in place for the regular and comprehensive acquisition of material from all places where Jewish Civilization is taught. Subsequent Inventories will be issued on a regular basis.

The second section of the Inventory lists syllabi now in our collection. In order to facilitate its use, syllabi are listed alphabetically by author and then indexed by subject area. It should be understood that the syllabi listed here vary considerably in scope, detail and quality. They enter the World Register as submitted, untouched by the editor's pen. Moreover, many of the most instructive syllabi used in universities around the world have not yet been contributed to the collection. The World Register continues to grow, and subsequent issues of the Inventory will list the syllabi which we hope will be added to our archive in the coming years.

The World Register's holdings can be consulted in two ways. Colleagues are welcome to visit the offices of the International Center in Jerusalem, where the World Register is open to them for their use. If a personal visit is not possible, we shall be happy to respond to reasonably specific requests by sending (at cost) photocopies or summaries of material to those who can benefit from them.

No claim is made for the comprehensiveness of our holdings. Although the World Register is the only global collection of material on the teaching of Jewish Civilization now available, much material remains to be added. The Inventory is issued at this point so that the World Register can provide service to the field even in its incomplete state.

The third section of this Inventory comprises an analysis of the courses in Jewish history which are now listed in the World Register. In each issue of the Inventory, we plan to analyze some area in the teaching of Jewish Civilization in order to share with colleagues some of what can be learned about the field when systematic data are use to supplement personal impressions.

The preparation of this Inventory involved the participation of several people, whose assistance we gratefully acknowledge. Florinda Goldberg organized the material and undertook the painstaking task of proofreading the typescript. Patricia Redifer prepared the material for publication. Naomi Linder Kahn, Theodore Marcus, and Matthew Kalman prepared the data on Jewish history courses for computer analysis. Moshe Davis and Natan Lerner read the entire manuscript and made several helpful suggestions.

It is our hope that the World Register will serve to enhance the teaching of Jewish Civilization in institutions of higher learning. We also hope that our colleagues will send us their additions, reactions and suggestions. As is the case with most academic enterprises, the World Register will grow best in cooperation with those whom it serves.

M.F.V.

Jerusalem
April, 1985

PART ONE

Institutions

INSTITUTIONS OF HIGHER LEARNING THAT TEACH JEWISH CIVILIZATION

The World Register's source material for each institution is indicated by the following codes:

B   The institution publishes a brochure, available in the World Register, about its offerings in Jewish Civilization

Bm   The institution publishes a substantive magazine in Jewish Civilization. Copy is in the World Register

D   The institution has a separate Department of Judaic (or Jewish) Studies

F   The names of instructors of courses in Jewish Civilization are listed in the World Register

G   Information about graduate courses in Jewish Civilization is in the World Register

P   The institution has a special program in Jewish Civilization

Sc   The World Register has a complete collection of the institution's syllabi or course descriptions in Jewish Civilization

Sp   The World Register has a partial collection of the institution's syllabi or course descriptions in Jewish Civilization

Tc   The World Register has a complete collection of the institution's course titles in Jewish Civilization

Tp   The World Register has a partial collection of the institution's course titles in Jewish Civilization

For ease of reference, these codes are repeated on the inside back cover.

ARGENTINA

Universidad Nacional de Buenos Aires	Tc	F	
Universidad de Belgrano, Buenos Aires	Tc	Sp	F
Universidad Nacional de Rosario	Tc	F	
Universidad del Salvador, Buenos Aires	Tc	F	
Universidad Nacional del Sur, Bahía Blanca	Tp		

AUSTRALIA

A.C.T.

Australian National University, Canberra	Tp

NEW SOUTH WALES

University of New England, Armidale	G	Tp		
University of New South Wales, Kensington	Tc	Sc	F	
University of Sydney	P	Tc	Sc	F

QUEENSLAND

University of Queensland, St. Lucia	Tp

VICTORIA

Institute of Catholic Education, Melbourne	Tc				
La Trobe University, Bundoora	G	Tc	F		
University of Melbourne, Parkville	G	Tc	Sc	F	B
Monash University, Clayton	G	Tp	Sp		
Victoria College					
Rusden Campus, Clayton	Tc	Sc			
Toorak Campus, Malvern	D	Tc	Sc	F	

WESTERN AUSTRALIA

University of Western Australia, Needlands   Tp

AUSTRIA

Universität Wien - Institut für Judaistik   D G Tc Sc F

BELGIUM

Institut Martin Buber, Bruxelles   D Tc Sc F
Université de Louvain   G Tc F

BRAZIL

Universidade Católica, Rio de Janeiro   Tp
Universidade do Estado de Rio de Janeiro   P Tc Sc F
Universidade Estadual de Campinas   Tc F
Universidade Federal do Rio de Janeiro   Tp
Pontifícia Universidade Católica de
  Minas Gerais   Tc
Pontifícia Universidade Católica de
  São Paulo   Tc Sp F
Universidade de São Paulo   P Tc Sc F Bm

CANADA

ALBERTA

University of Alberta, Edmonton   Tp
University of Calgary   G Tc Sc F
University of Lethbridge   Tc Sc

BRITISH COLUMBIA

University of British Columbia, Vancouver	G	Tc	Sc	F
Capilano College, Vancouver	Tp			
Langara College, Vancouver	Tp			
Union College of British Columbia	Tp			

MANITOBA

Brandon University	Tc	F		
University of Manitoba, Winnipeg	D	Tc	Sc	F
University of Winnipeg	Tp			

NEW BRUNSWICK

Mount Allison University, Sackville	Tc	Sc	F
University of New Brunswick, Fredericton	Tp		
Saint Jerome's College	Tc	Sc	

NEWFOUNDLAND

Memorial University, St. John's	Tc	Sc	F

NOVA SCOTIA

Dalhousie University, Halifax	Tc	Sc	F
University of King's College, Halifax	Tp		
Saint Mary's University, Halifax	Tc	Sc	F

ONTARIO

Carleton University, Ottawa	Tc	Sc	
Humber College of Applied Arts and Technology, Rexdale	F		
Huron College, London	Tc	Sc	F

ONTARIO (continued)

Laurentian University of Sudbury	Tp				
McMaster University, Hamilton	Tp	Sp	F		
University of Ottawa	Tc	Sc	F		
Saint Paul University, Ottawa	Tp				
University of Toronto	P	G	Tc	Sc	F
University of Waterloo	Tp	Sp			
University of Western Ontario, London	Tc	Sc			
Wilfrid Laurier University, Waterloo	G	Tc	Sc	F	
University of Windsor	Tp				
York University, Downsview	Tp	Sp	F		

QUEBEC

Bishop's University, Lennoxville	Tc	Sc			
Concordia University, Montreal	P	G	Tc	Sc	F
Dawson College, Montreal	P	Tc	Sc	F	
John Abbott College, Ste. Anne de Bellevue	Tp				
Université Laval, Quebec City	Tc	Sc	F		
Loyola of Montreal	F				
McGill University, Montreal	P	G	Tc	Sc	F
Université de Montréal	P	Tc	Sc	F	
Queen's University, Queen's Theological College, Kingston	Tp	Sp			
Université de Sherbrooke	Tp				
Sir George Williams University, Montreal	G	Tc	Sc		
Vanier College, Montreal	Tp	F			

SASKATCHEWAN

University of Regina	Tc	Sc	
University of Saskatchewan, Saskatoon	Tc	Sc	F

CHILE

Universidad de Chile, Santiago   Tc Sp F

COLOMBIA

Universidad Javeriana, Bogotá   Tc F

COSTA RICA

Universidad de Costa Rica, San José   Tp F

DENMARK

Aarhus Universitet   Tc Sc F

Københavns Universitet   Tc F

FINLAND

Åbo Academi   Tc Sc F

Helsingfors Universitet   Tc F

FRANCE

Université de Besançon   Tp

Université de Bordeaux III   P Tp F

Centre National de la Recherche
  Scientifique, Paris   P Tc F

College de France, Paris   Tc F

Ecole des Hautes Etudes en Sciences
  Sociales, Paris   P Tp F

Ecole Pratique des Hautes Etudes, Paris   Tc F

Université François Rabelais, Tours   P Tp F

Université des Langues et Lettres de
  Grenoble   Tp

FRANCE (continued)

Institut National des Langues et Civilisations Orientales (Université de Paris III)	P	G	Tc	F	B	Bm
Université de Lille III	P	Tp	Sp	F		
Université de Lyon II	Tp					
Université de Lyon III	P	G	Tc	F		
Université de Nancy II	P	Tc	F			
Université de Nice	Tc	F				
Université de Paris I	P	Tc	F			
Université de Paris II	G					
Université de Paris III - Sorbonne Nouvelle	P	G	Tc	F		
Université de Paris VII	P	G	F			
Université de Paris VIII	D	G	Tc	Sc	F	
Université de Paris X, Nanterre	Tp	F				
Université de Paris XII, Créteil Val-de-Marne	Tp	F				
Université Paul Valéry (Montpellier III)	P	Tc	F			
Université de Provence (Centre d'Aix)	P	Tp	F			
Université des Sciences Humaines, Strasbourg	D	G	Tc	F		
Université de Toulouse II	P	Tp	F			

FEDERAL REPUBLIC OF GERMANY

Universität Duisburg	Tc	F			
Hochschule für Jüdische Studien, Heidelberg	P	G	Tc	Sp	F
Universität zu Köln	P	G	Tc	F	
Rheinische Friedrich-Wilhelms Universität, Bonn	Tc	F			
Ruprecht-Karls Universität, Heidelberg	Tc	F			

GUATEMALA

Universidad Mariano Gálvez, Guatemala	Tc	Sc

13

ICELAND

Háskóli Íslands (University of
   Iceland), Reykjavík   Tc   F

REPUBLIC OF IRELAND

Dublin University (Trinity College)	P	Tc		F
University College, Dublin		Tc	Sc	F

ITALY

Facoltà Teologica de Italia Settentrionale, Milano		Tp		F
Facoltà Valdese de Teologia, Roma		Tp		
Istituto Universitario Orientale, Napoli	P	Tc	Sc	F
Pontificia Facoltà Teologica di San Bonaventura – Seraphicum, Roma		Tc	Sc	F
Pontificio Istituto Biblico, Roma		Tc		
Pontificio Istituto Liturgico, Roma		Tp		
Pontificia Università Gregoriana, Roma	P	Tc		
Pontificia Università Lateranense, Roma		Tc		F
Università Pontificia Salesiana, Roma		Tc		F
Pontificia Università Urbaniana, Roma		Tc	Sc	F
Seminario di Lingua e Letteratura Ebraica, Roma		Tp		
Università Cattolica del Sacro Cuore, Milano		Tp		
Università degli Studi di Bologna		Tc		
Università degli Studi di Firenze		Tc		
Università degli Studi di Genova		Tp		
Università degli Studie di Padova		Tc	Sc	F
Università di Pavia		Tc	Sc	F
Università degli Studi di Roma		Tp		F
Università degli Studi – Ca'Foscari, Venezia		Tc	Sc	F

MEXICO

El Colegio de México, Mexico	Tp					
Universidad Iberoamericana, Mexico	P	G	Tc	Sc	F	B
Universidad Nacional Autónoma de México, Mexico	Tp					

THE NETHERLANDS

Universiteit van Amsterdam - Juda Palache Instituut	P	G	Tc	F	B	
Rijksuniversiteit te Groningen	G	Tc	Sc	F		
Rijksuniversiteit te Leiden	Tp	F				
Rijksuniversiteit te Utrecht	G	Tc	Sc	F		
Hogeschool te Tilburg	Tp					
Katholieke Hogeschool Amsterdam	Tp	F				
Katholieke Hogeschool Nijmegen	P	Tc	Sc			
Katholieke Hogeschool Utrecht	Tp	F				

NORWAY

Misjonshøgskolen I Stavanger	Tc	F	
Universitetet I Oslo	Tc	F	
Det Teologiske Menighetsfakultet I Oslo	Tc	F	B
Universitetet I Trondheim-Norges Laererhøgskole	Tc	F	

PANAMA

Universidad de Panamá	Tp

PHILIPPINES

Women's University of the Philippines, Manila	Tc

POLAND

Uniwersytet Jagiellonsky, Krakow	Tp	F
Uniwersytet Warszawski, Warsaw	Tp	F
Katolicki Uniwersytet Lubelski, Lublin	Tp	F

PORTUGAL

Universidade de Coimbra	Tp	F
Universidade Nova de Lisboa	Tp	F

SOUTH AFRICA

University of Cape Town	D	G	Tc	Sc	F	B
University of Durban-Westville, Durban	Tc					
University of Fort Hare, Alice	G	Tp				
University of Natal, Durban	D	G	Tc	Sc	F	
University of the North, Pietersburg	Tp					
University of the Orange Free State, Bloemfontein	Tp					
University of Port Elizabeth	P	G	Tc			
Potchefstroomse Universiteit vir C.H.O.	Tc	Sc				
Universiteit van Pretoria	Tc	Sc				
Rand Afrikaans University, Johannesburg	Tp					
Rhodes University, Grahamstown	P	Tc	Sc			
University of South Africa (UNISA), Pretoria	G	Tc	Sc	F		
University of Stellenbosch	Tc					
University of Western Cape, Cape Town	Tp	Sp				
University of the Witwatersrand, Johannesburg	D	G	Tc	Sc	F	

16

SPAIN

Universidad de Barcelona	D	F		
Universidad de Comillas, Madrid	Tp			
Universidad Complutense de Madrid	D	Tc	Sc	F
Universidad de Granada	D	Tc	Sc	F
Universidad Pontificia de Salamanca	D	F		

SWEDEN

Göteborgs Universitet	Tc	
Lunds Universitet	Tc	F
Stockholms Universitet	Tc	F
Uppsala Universitet	Tc	F

SWITZERLAND

Université de Fribourg	G	Tc	F
Theologische Fakultät Luzern	G	Tc	F

UNITED KINGDOM

ENGLAND

Birmingham University	Tp	F			
University of Bristol	Tp				
Cambridge University	P	Tc	Sp	F	
Durham University	P	Tc	Sc	F	
Exeter University	P	Tp	Sp	F	
University of Hull	Tp				
University of Kent at Canterbury	Tp				
University of Lancaster	Tp	F			
Leeds University	P	G	Tp	Sp	F
University of Leicester	Tp	Sp			

ENGLAND (continued)

University of Liverpool	P	Tp				
London University	P	G	Tc	Sc	F	
Manchester University	Tp	F				
Middlesex Polytechnic, London	D	Tp	F			
University of Newcastle-upon-Tyne	Tp					
Oxford University	P	G	Tc	Sc	F	Bm
University of Salford	Tp					
University of Stirling	Tp					
Sunderland Polytechnic	Tp					
University of Sussex, Brighton	Tp					
Trinity College, Bristol	Tp					
University College, London	P	G	Tc	Sc	F	
University of Warwick	Tc	Sc	F			

NORTHERN IRELAND

The Queen's University of Belfast	P	Tc	Sp	F

SCOTLAND

Aberdeen University	D	G	Tc	Sp	F
Edinburgh University	G	Tc	F		
Glasgow University	D	G	Tc	Sc	F
New College, Edinburgh	D	F			
Saint Andrews University, Fife	G	Tp	Sp	F	

WALES

University College, Cardiff	P	Tp	F
University College of North Wales, Bangor	Tp		
University of Wales, Saint David's College Lampeter	Tp		

UNITED STATES

ALABAMA

University of Alabama, University	Tp
Birmingham Southern College	Tp
Florence State University	Tp
Spring Hill College, Mobile	Tp

ARIZONA

Arizona State University, Tempe	Tp	F	
Phoenix College	Tp		
University of Arizona, Tucson	P	G	Tp

CALIFORNIA

Alan Hancock College, Santa Maria	Tp	
Ambassador College, Pasadena	Tp	
American Baptist Seminary of the West, Berkeley	Tc	F
Azusa Pacific College	Tc	
Bakersfield College	Tc	
Bethany Bible College, Santa Cruz	Tc	
Biola College, La Mirada	Tc	
Cabrillo College, Aptos	Tc	
California Baptist College, Riverside	Tc	
California Christian College, Fresno	Tc	
California Polytechnic State University San Luis Obispo	Tc	

CALIFORNIA (continued)

California State University System (CSU)

CSU at Chico	Tp	Sp	F		
CSU Dominguez Hills, Carson	Tc				
CSU at Fresno	Tc				
CSU at Fullerton	Tc	Sc	F		
CSU at Hayward	G	Tc	Sc	F	
CSU at Long Beach	Tc	Sc	F		
CSU at Northridge	P	Tc	Sc	F	
CSU at Sacramento	Tp				
CSU at Stanislaus, Furlock	Tp	Sp			
San Diego State University (CSU)	P	Tc	Sc	F	
San Francisco State University (CSU)	Tp	Sp	F		
San Jose State University (CSU)	P	Tc	Sc	F	B
Sonoma State University (CSU)	Tc				

University of California (UC)

UC at Berkeley	P	G	Tc	Sc
UC at Davis	Tc			
UC at Irvine	Tp			
UC at Los Angeles (UCLA)	P	G	Tc	Sp
UC at Riverside	Tc			
UC at San Diego	P	Tc	Sc	F	B
UC at Santa Barbara	Tc			
UC at Santa Cruz	Tc			

Canada College, Redwood City	Tc
Chapman College, Orange	Tc
Christ College, Irvine	Tc
Christian Heritage College, El Cajon	Tc

CALIFORNIA (continued)

Claremont College System (CCS)
    Claremont Men's College (CCS)   Tp
    Pitzer College (CCS)   Tc
    Pomona College (CCS)   Tc Sc F

Claremont Graduate School   Tc
Claremont McKenna College   Tc
Coastime Community College   Tc
College of Notre Dame, Belmont   Tc
Cypress College   Tc
Dominican College, San Rafael   Tc
Dominican School of Philosophy and Theology,
  Berkeley   Tc
Foothill College, Los Altos Hills   Tc
Fresno Pacific College   Tc
Golden Gate Baptist Theological Seminary,   G Tc Sc F
  Mill Valley
Golden West College, Huntington Beach   Tc
Graduate Theological Union, Berkeley   P G Tc Sc F
Grossmount College, El Cajon   Tc
Harvey Mudd College, Claremont   Tp
Holy Family College, Fremont   Tc
Imperial Valley College   Tc
Laney College, Oakland   Tc
Life Bible College, Los Angeles   Tc
Loma Linda University   Tc
Long Beach City College   Tc
Los Angeles Baptist College, Newhall   Tc Sc

CALIFORNIA (continued)

Los Angeles City College System
    East Los Angeles College   Tc Sp
    Los Angeles City College   Tc
    Los Angeles Harbor College, Wilmington   Tc
    Los Angeles Pierce College,
      Woodland Hills   Tc Sc F
    Los Angeles Valley College, Van Nuys   P Tc Sc   F
    West Los Angeles College, Culver City   Tc

Los Angeles Mission College, San Fernando   Tc
Los Angeles Southwest College   Tc
Loyola-Marymount College, Los Angeles   Tc
Mendocino College, Ukiah   Tc
Mennonite Brethren Biblical Seminary,
  Fresno   Tc
Merritt College, Oakland   Tc
Mills College, Oakland   Tc
Mission College, Santa Clara   Tc
Moorpark College   Tc
Mt. Saint Antonio College, Walnut   Tc
Occidental College, Los Angeles   Tc Sc F
Orange Coast College, Costa Mesa   Tc Sc
Pacific Christian College, Fullerton   Tc
Pacific School of Religion, Berkeley   Tc
Pacific Union College, Anawin   Tc
University of the Pacific, Stockton   Tc
Palomar College, San Marcos   P Tc
Pasadena City College   Tc Sp
Patten College, Oakland   Tc Sc F

Pepperdine University, Malibu	Tc			
Point Loma College, San Diego	Tc			
Sacramento City College	Tc	Sp		
Saddleback College, Mission Viejo	Tc			
Saint Mary's College of California, Moraga	Tc			
San Bernardino Valley College	Tc			
San Diego City College	Tc			
San Diego Mesa College	Tc			
University of San Francisco	P	Tc		
San Joaquin Delta College, Stockton	Tc			
San Jose Bible College	Tc			
Santa Ana College	Tc			
Santa Barbara City College	Tc			
Santa Monica College	Tc	Sp		
School of Theology at Claremont	Tc			
Scripps College, Claremont	Tp			
Skyline College, San Bruno	Tp			
Southern California College, Costa Mesa	Tp			
University of Southern California, Los Angeles	P	G	Tp	Sp
Stanford University	Tc	Sp	F	
Taft College	Tc			
Talbot Theological Seminary, La Mirada	Tc			
Thomas Starr King School, Berkeley	Tc			
University of La Verne	Tc			
West Valley College, Saratoga	Tc			
Whittier College	Tc			

COLORADO

Colorado State University, Ft. Collins	Tp					
University of Colorado, Boulder	Tp					
University of Denver	P	G	Tc	Sc	F	B
Regis College, Denver	Tp					

CONNECTICUT

Albertus Magnus College, New Haven	Tp					
University of Bridgeport	Tp					
University of Connecticut (UCon)						
UCon at Stamford	D	Tp	F			
UCon at Storrs	D	Tc	Sc	F	B	
UCon at West Hartford	Tp	Sp	F			
Connecticut College, New London	Tc	Sc				
Greater Hartford Community College, Hartford	Tp					
University of Hartford, West Hartford	Tp					
Quinnipiac College, New Haven	Tp					
Sacred Heart University, Bridgeport	Tp					
Trinity College, Hartford	Tp					
Wesleyan University, Middletown	P	Tp	Sp			
Yale University, New Haven	P	G	Tc	Sc	F	B

DELAWARE

University of Delaware, Newark	Tp					

DISTRICT OF COLUMBIA
(Washington, D.C.)

The American University	P	Tc	Sp	F	B
Catholic University of America	Tp				

DISTRICT OF COLUMBIA (continued)

Gallaudet College	Tp				
Georgetown University	Tp				
George Washington University	P	G	Tp	F	
Howard University	Tp				
Trinity College	Tp				
Wesley Theological Seminary	G	Tc	Sc	F	B

FLORIDA

Barry College, Miami Shores	Tp				
Bethune-Cookman College, Daytona Beach	Tp				
State University System of Florida (SUSF)					
University of Florida, Gainesville (SUSF)	P	Tc	Sc	F	B
Florida Atlantic University, Boca Raton (SUSF)	Tp				
Florida International University, Miami (SUSF)	Tp				
Florida State University, Tallahassee (SUSF)	Tp				
University of South Florida, Tampa (SUSF)	Tp				
Jacksonville University	Tp				
University of Miami, Coral Gables	P	Tc	Sc	F	B
Miami-Dade Community College					
Miami (South Campus)	Tp				
Coral Gables (North Campus)	Tp				
University of Tampa	Tp				

GEORGIA

Berry College, Mt. Berry	Tp				
Emory University, Atlanta	P	G	Tc	Sc	F	B

25

GEORGIA (continued)

University of Georgia, Athens	Tp			
Georgia Institute of Technology, Atlanta	Tp			
Georgia State University, Atlanta	Tp			

HAWAII

University of Hawaii at Manoa, Honolulu	P			

ILLINOIS

Augustana College, Rock Island	Tp				
Barat College, Lake Forest	Tp				
Bethany Theological Seminary, Oak Park	Tp	Sp	F		
Bradley University, Peoria	Tp				
Chicago Theological Seminary	Tp	Sp	F		
City College of Chicago	Tp				
University of Chicago	G	Tc	Sp	F	
De Paul University, Chicago	Tp				
Garrett Evangelical Theological Seminary, Evanston	Tp	Sp	F		
University of Illinois					
Chicago Circle Campus	D	G	Tp	Sp	F
Urbana Campus	P	Tc	Sp	F	B
Illinois Wesleyan University, Bloomington	Tp				
Lake Forest College	Tp				
The Loop College, Chicago	Tp				
Loyola University, Chicago	Tp				
Lutheran School of Theology, Chicago	Tp	Sp	F		
Northeastern Illinois University, Chicago	P	Tc	Sc	F	

ILLINOIS (continued)

Northern Illinois University, DeKalb	Tp			
North Park Theological Seminary, Chicago	Tp	Sp	F	
Northwestern University, Evanston	Tc	Sc	F	
Roosevelt University, Chicago	Tp			
Saint Xavier College, Chicago	Tp			
Southern Illinois University, Carbondale	G	Tp	Sp	F

INDIANA

Associated Mennonite Biblical Seminaries, Elkhart	Tc	Sc	F		
Butler University, Indianapolis	Tp				
Calumet College, Whiting	Tp				
Concordia Senior College, Fort Wayne	Tp				
Earlham College, Richmond	Tp				
Grace College, Winona Lake	Tc	Sc	F		
Indiana State University, Terra Haute	Tp				
Indiana University, Bloomington	P	Tp	Sp	F	B
Indiana University-Southeast, New Albany	Tp				
Manchester College, North Manchester	Tp	Sp	F		
Marian College, Indianapolis	Tp				
University of Notre Dame	G	Tc	Sp	F	
Purdue University, Lafayette	P	Tp	Sp	F	B
Saint Meinrad College	Tc	Sc	F		
Taylor University, Upland	Tp				
Valparaiso University	P	Tp	F		
Wabash College, Cramfordsville	Tp	Sp			

IOWA

Drake University, Des Moines	Tp	
Grinnell College	Tp	
Iowa State University of Science and Technology, Ames	Tp	
University of Iowa, Iowa City	Tp	
Luther College, Decorah	Tp	
Morningside College, Sioux City	Tp	
Northwestern College, Orange City	Tp	Sp
Westman College, Le Mars	Tp	

KANSAS

University of Kansas, Lawrence	Tp	
Kansas State University, Manhattan	Tp	
Wichita State University	Tp	F

KENTUCKY

Asbury College, Wilmore	Tp			
Bellarmine-Ursuline College, Louisville	Tc	Sc	F	
Centre College of Kentucky, Danville	Tc	Sc		
Georgetown College	Tp			
University of Kentucky, Lexington	D	Tc	Sc	F
University of Louisville	Tc	Sc	F	
Louisville Presbyterian Theological Seminary	Tc	Sc	F	
Murray State University	Tp	Sp	F	
Southern Baptist Theological Seminary, Louisville	G	Tc	Sc	F
Sue Bennett College, London	Tp	Sp	F	
Western Kentucky University, Bowling Green	Tp	Sp	F	

28

LOUISIANA

Louisiana State University, Baton Rouge	Tp			
Loyola University, New Orleans	Tp			
University of New Orleans	Tp			
Tulane University, New Orleans	Tp	Sp	F	Bm

MAINE

Bowdoin College, Brunswick	Tp	
Colby College, Waterville	Tp	F
University of Maine, Orono	Tp	

MARYLAND

Community College of Baltimore	Tp					
University of Baltimore	Tp					
Goucher College, Towson	Tp					
Johns Hopkins University, Baltimore	G	Tp				
Loyola College, Baltimore	Tp					
University of Maryland						
Baltimore County Campus	Tp					
College Park Campus	P	G	Tc	Sc	F	B
Towson State University, Baltimore	P	G	Tc	Sc	F	

MASSACHUSETTS

American International College, Springfield	Tp					
Amherst College	Tp					
Boston College, Chestnut Hill	Tp					
Boston State College	Tp					
Boston University	P	G	Tp	Sp	F	B

29

MASSACHUSETTS (continued)

Brandeis University, Waltham	D	G	Tc	Sc	F	
Bunker Hill Community College	Tp					
Clark University, Worcester	D	Tc	Sc	F		
College of the Holy Cross, Worcester	Tp					
Emerson College, Brookline	Tp	Sp	F			
Emmanuel College, Boston	Tp					
Gordon College, Wenham	Tp					
Hampshire College, Amherst	Tp	Sp	F			
Harvard University and Radcliffe College, Cambridge	D	G	Tc	Sp	F	B
Harvard Divinity School	Tp	Sp				
Lasell Junior College, Aubrundale	Tp					
Lesley College, Cambridge	Tp					
University of Lowell	Tp	Sp	F			
Massachusetts Institute of Technology, Cambridge	Tp					
University of Massachusetts						
Amherst Campus	P	Tp				
Boston Campus	Tp					
Merrimack College, North Andover	Tp					
Mount Holyoke College, South Hadley	Tp					
Northeastern University, Boston	Tp					
Salem State College	Tp					
Simmons College, Boston	Tp	Sp	F			
Smith College, Northampton	P	Tc	F			
Southeastern Massachusetts University, North Dartmouth	Tp	F				
Springfield College	Tp					
Stonehill College	Tp					

MASSACHUSETTS (continued)

Tufts University, Medford	Tp	F			
Wellesley College	Tp				
Wheaton College, Norton	Tp				
Williams College, Williamstown	Tp	Sp	F		

MICHIGAN

Andrews University, Berrien Springs	Tp				
University of Detroit	Tc	Sc	F		
Mercy College of Detroit	Tp				
Michigan State University, East Lansing	P	Tc	Sc	F	
University of Michigan, Ann Arbor	P	G	Tc	Sc	F
Oakland University, Rochester	Tp				
Wayne State University, Detroit	P	Tp			
Western Michigan University, Kalamazoo	Tp				

MINNESOTA

Augsburg College, Minneapolis	Tp				
Carleton College, Northfield	Tp	Sp	F		
Concordia College, Moorhead	Tp				
Hamline College, St. Paul	Tp				
Macalester College, St. Paul	Tc	Sc	F		
University of Minnesota					
Duluth Campus	Tp	Sp	F		
Minneapolis Campus	P	Tp	Sp	F	B
College of Saint Catherine, St. Paul	Tp				

MINNESOTA (continued)

Saint John's University, Collegeville	Tp		
Saint Olaf College and Paracollege, Northfield	Tp	Sp	F
College of Saint Thomas, St. Paul	Tp		

MISSOURI

University of Missouri				
Kansas City Campus	P	G	Tp	Sp
St. Louis Campus	Tp			
Northeast Missouri State University, Kirksville	Tp			
Saint Louis University	Tp			
Seminex, St. Louis	Tp	Sp	F	
Washington University, St. Louis	P	Tc	Sc	F B
Webster College, St. Louis	Tp			
Westminster College, Fulton	Tp			

MONTANA

Big Sky Bible College	Tc	Sc
Carroll College, Helena	Tc	Sc
College of Great Falls	Tc	Sc
Dawson College, Glendive	Tc	Sc
Flathead Valley Community College, Kalispell	Tc	Sc
Miles Community College, Miles City	Tc	Sc
Montana State University, Bozeman	Tc	Sc
Northern Montana College, Haure	Tc	Sc
Rocky Mountain College, Billings	Tc	Sc
University of Montana, Missoula	Tc	Sc

NEBRASKA

Bellevue College	Tc	Sc	F	
College of Saint Mary, Omaha	Tc	Sc		
Concordia Teachers College, Seward	G	Tc		
Creighton University, Omaha	G	Tc	Sc	
Dana College, Blair	Tc	Sc		
Grace College of the Bible, Omaha	Tc			
Hastings College	Tc	Sc		
Kearney State College	Tc	Sc		
Midland Lutheran College, Fremont	Tc	Sc		
University of Nebraska				
Lincoln Campus	G	Tc	Sc	
Omaha Campus	G	Tc	Sc	
Nebraska Christian College	Tc	Sc		
Nebraska Indian Community College	Tc	Sc		
Nebraska Wesleyan University, Lincoln	Tc	Sc		
Nebraska Western College, Scottsbluff	Tc	Sc		
Peru State College	Tc	Sc		
Platte Bible College	Tc	Sc		
Saint Mary's University, Omaha	Tp			
Wayne State College	Tc	Sc	F	

NEW HAMPSHIRE

Dartmouth College, Hanover	Tp	Sp	F	B
New England College, Henniker	Tp			

NEW JERSEY

Caldwell College	Tp				
Drew University, Madison	G	Tp	Sp	F	

Farleigh Dickinson University

Madison Campus	Tp	
Teaneck Campus	Tp	

Jersey City State College	Tp				
Kean College, Union	P	Tc			
Luther College, Teaneck	Tp				
Princeton University	Tc	Sc	F	B	

Rutgers, State University of New
  Jersey

Camden Campus	Tp			
Newark Campus	Tc	Sc		
New Brunswick Campus	D	Tc	Sc	F

College of Saint Elizabeth, Convent Station	Tp				
Saint Peter's College, Jersey City	Tp				
Seton Hall University, South Orange	D	G	Tc	Sc	F
Trenton State College	Tp				
Upsala College, East Orange	Tp	Sp	F		

NEW MEXICO

University of Albuquerque	Tp		
Eastern New Mexico University, Portales	Tp		
University of New Mexico, Albuquerque	Tc	Sc	F

34

NEW YORK

Adelphi University, Garden City	Tp					
Alfred University	Tp					
Bard College, Annandale-on-Hudson	Tp					
Canisius College, Buffalo	Tp					
City University of New York System (CUNY)						
CUNY-Bernard Baruch College, New York	Tp					
CUNY-Brooklyn College	D	G	Tc	Sc	F	B
CUNY-City College of New York	D					
CUNY-Hunter College, New York	P	G				
CUNY-Lehman College, Bronx	P	Tc	Sc			
CUNY-Queens College, Flushing	P	G	Tc	Sc	F	B
CUNY-York College, Jamaica	P					
City University Community Colleges						
CUNY-Bronx Community College	Tp					
CUNY-Kingsborough Community College, Brooklyn	Tp					
CUNY-Manhattan Community College, New York	Tp					
CUNY-Queensborough Community College Bayside	Tp					
Colgate University, Hamilton	Tp					
Columbia University and Barnard College, New York	P	G	Tc	Sp	F	B
Cornell University, Ithaca	P	G	Tc	Sc		
D'Youville College, Buffalo	Tp					
Elmira College	Tp					
Fordham University, Bronx	Tp					
Hamilton College, Clinton	Tp	Sp				
Hilbert College, Hamburg	Tp					
Hobart and William Smith Colleges, Geneva	P	Tc	Sc	F		

35

NEW YORK (continued)

Hofstra University, Hempstead	P					
Houghton College	Tp					
Iona College, New Rochelle	Tp					
Ithaca College	Tp					
Le Moyne College, Syracuse	Tp					
Long Island University, Brooklyn Center and C.W. Post Center, Greenvale	P	Tp	Sp	F		
Manhattan College, Bronx	Tp					
Manhattanville College, Purchase	Tp					
Marist College, Poughkeepsie	Tp					
Marymount College, Tarrytown	Tp					
Marymount Manhattan College, New York	Tp					
Mercy College, New Rochelle	Tp					
Molloy College, Rockville Center	Tp					
College of Mount St. Vincent, Riverdale	Tp	Sp				
Nazareth College, Rochester	Tp					
College of New Rochelle	Tp					
New School for Social Research, New York	Tc	F	B			
New York Institute of Technology, Westbury	Tp					
New York University	P	G	Tc	Sc	F	B
Pace University, New York	Tp	F				
University of Rochester	Tp	F				
Russell Sage College, Troy	Tp					
Saint Benaventure University	Tp					
Saint Francis College, Brooklyn	Tp					
Saint John's University, Jamaica	Tp					
Saint John Fisher College, Rochester	Tp	F				
College of Saint Rose, Albany	Tp					
Sarah Lawrence College, Bronxville	Tp					

NEW YORK (continued)

Siena College, Loudonville	Tp					

State University of New York (SUNY)

SUNY at Albany	D	G	Tc	Sc	F	
SUNY at Binghamton	P	Tc	Sc	F	B	
SUNY at Buffalo	P	Tc	Sc	F	B	
SUNY at Stony Brook	P	Tp	F			

State University Colleges

SUNY College at Brockport	Tp			
SUNY College at Buffalo	Tp			
SUNY College at New Paltz	Tp			
SUNY College at Old Westbury	Tp			
SUNY College at Oneonta	P	Tc	Sc	B
SUNY College at Purchase	Tp			
SUNY-Nassau Community College, Garden City	Tp			

Syracuse University	P	Tp	Sp	F	B
Touro College	G	Tp			
Union College, Schenectady	Tp				
Vassar College, Poughkeepsie	Tc	Sc	F		
Wells College, Aurora	Tp				
Yeshiva University	D	G	Tc	Sc	F	Bm

NORTH CAROLINA

Appalachian State University, Boone	Tp				
Davidson College	Tp				
Duke University, Durham	P	G	Tp	Sp	B
Greensboro College	Tp				

NORTH CAROLINA (continued)

Lenoir Rhyne College, Hickory	Tp			
University of North Carolina, Chapel Hill	Tc	Sc	F	
Wake Forest University, Winston Salem	Tp			

NORTH DAKOTA

Bismarck Junior College	Tc	Sc		
Mary College, Bismarck	Tc	Sc		
Mayville State College	Tc	Sc		
Minot State College	Tc	Sc		
University of North Dakota				
Grand Forks	Tc	Sc		
Williston Center	Tc	Sc		
North Dakota State University, Fargo	G	Tc	Sc	
Trinity Bible Institute, Ellendale	Tc	Sc		
Valley City State College	Tc	Sc		

OHIO

Antioch College, Yellow Springs	Tp				
Baldwin Wallace College, Berea	Tp				
Bowling Green State University	Tp	Sp	F		
Capital University, Columbus	Tp				
Case-Western Reserve University, Cleveland	Tc	Sc	F		
University of Cincinnati	P	Tc	Sp	F	B
Cleveland State University	Tp				
Cuyahoga Community College, Cleveland	Tp				
University of Dayton	Tp				
Denison University, Granville	Tp	F			
Edgecliff College, Cincinnati	Tp				

OHIO (continued)

Hiram College	Tp					
John Carroll University, Cleveland	Tp					
Kent State University	Tp					
Kenyon College, Gambier	Tp					
Marietta College	Tp					
Mary Manse College, Toledo	Tp					
Miami University, Oxford	Tp					
Oberlin College	P	Tc				
Ohio State University, Columbus	P	G	Tc	Sc	F	B
Ohio University, Athens	Tp					
Ohio Wesleyan, Delaware	Tp					
University of Toledo	Tp					
Walsh College, Canton	Tp					
College of Wooster	Tp					
Wright State University	Tp	F				
Xavier University, Cincinnati	Tp					
Youngstown State University	Tp					

OKLAHOMA

Oklahoma City College	Tp
Oklahoma State University, Stillwater	Tp
University of Oklahoma, Norman	Tp
University of Tulsa	Tp

OREGON

Concordia College, Portland	Tc		
George Fox College, Newberg	Tc	Sc	F
Lewis and Clark College, Portland	Tc	Sc	F
Linfield College, McMinnville	Tc		

OREGON (continued)

Oregon State University, Corvallis	Tc	Sc	
University of Oregon, Eugene	Tc	Sc	
Pacific University, Forest Grove	Tp	Sp	
Portland State University	Tp	F	
University of Portland	Tc	F	
Reed College, Portland	Tc	Sc	
Rogue Community College, Grants Pass	Tc		
Warner Pacific College, Portland	Tc	Sp	
Western Oregon State College, Monmouth	Tc	Sc	F
Willamette University, Salem	Tp	Sp	F

PENNSYLVANIA

Allegheny College, Meadville	Tp		
Bryn Mawr College, Haverford	P	Tp	Sp
Bucknell University, Lewisburg	Tp		
Carnegie-Mellon University, Pittsburgh	Tp		
Chatham College, Pittsburgh	Tp		
Community College of Philadelphia	Tp		
Dickinson College, Carlisle	P	Tp	
Drexel University, Philadelphia	Tp		
Duquesne University, Pittsburgh	Tp		
Franklin and Marshall Colelge, Lancaster	Tp		
Gettyburg College	Tp		
Gwynedd-Mercy College, Gwynedd Valley	Tp		
Haverford College	Tp		
King's College, Wilkes-Barre	Tp		
Kutztown State College	Tp	Sp	F
Lafayette College, Easton	Tc	Sc	F
La Salle College, Philadelphia	Tp		

PENNSLYVANIA (continued)

Lehigh University, Bethlehem	P	Tc	Sc	F
Lycoming College, Williamsport	Tp			
Marywood College, Scranton	Tp			
Messiah College, Grantham	Tp			
Millersville State College	Tp			
Muhlenberg College, Allentown	Tc	Sc	F	
University of Pennsylvania, Philadelphia	G	Tc	Sp	F
Pennsylvania State University, University Park	Tp	Sp	F	
University of Pittsburgh	P	Tp	Sp	F
Rosemont College	Tp			
Saint Joseph's College, Philadelphia	Tp			
Saint Vincent College, Latrobe	Tp			
University of Scranton	Tp			
Slippery Rock State College	Tp			
Susquehenna University, Selinsgrove	Tp			
Swarthmore College	Tp			
Temple University				
Ambler Campus	Tp			
Philadelphia Campus	P	G	Tp	Sp	F
Ursinus College, Collegeville	Tp			
Villanova University	Tp			
West Chester State College	Tp			
Widener College, Chester	Tp	F		
Wilson College, Chambersburg	Tp			

RHODE ISLAND

Brown University, Providence	P	G	Tc	Sc	F	Bm
Providence College	Tp					
University of Rhode Island, Kingston	Tp					

SOUTH CAROLINA

Clemson University	Tc
University of South Carolina, Columbia	Tp

SOUTH DAKOTA

Augustana College, Sioux Falls	Tc	Sc
Black Hills State College, Spearfish	Tc	Sc
Dakota Wesleyan University, Mitchell	Tc	Sc
Freeman Junior College	Tc	Sc
Mount Marty College	Tc	Sc
North American Baptist Seminary, Sioux Falls	Tc	Sc
Northern State College, Aberdeen	Tc	Sc
Presentation College, Aberdeen	Tc	Sc
Sioux Falls College	Tc	Sc
South Dakota State University, Brookings	Tc	Sc
University of South Dakota, Springfield	Tc	Sc
Yankton College	Tc	Sc

TENNESSEE

Belmont College, Nashville	Tc	F	
Bryan College, Dayton	Tc	Sp	
Davis Lipscomb College, Nashville	Tp		
Emmanuel School of Religion, Milligan College	Tc	Sc	
Free Will Baptist Bible College, Nashville	Tc	Sc	F
Harding Graduate School of Religion, Memphis	G	Tc	Sc	F
King College, Bristol	Tc	Sc	F

TENNESSEE (continued)

Lee College, Cleveland	Tc	Sc	F
Memphis Theological Seminary	Tp	Sp	F
Mid-America Baptist Theological Seminary, Memphis	Tp	Sp	F
Scarritt College, Nashville	Tp		
University of the South, Sewanee	Tc	Sc	
Southwestern at Memphis	Tp	Sp	
University of Tennessee, Knoxville	Tp	Sp	F
Vanderbilt University, Nashville	Tp	Sp	F

TEXAS

Abilene Christian University	Tc	
Ambassador College, Big Sanday	Tp	
Angelo State University, San Angelo	Tc	
Arlington Baptist College	Tc	Sc
Austin College, Sherman	Tc	Sc
Baylor University, Waco	Tc	Sc
Brookhaven College, Farmer's Branch	Tc	
East Texas State University	Tc	Sc
El Paso Community College	Tc	Sc
Frank Phillips College, Borger	Tc	Sc
Gulf Coast Bible College, Houstone	Tc	Sc
Hardin Simmons University, Abilene	Tc	Sc
Henderson County Junior College, Athens	Tc	Sc
University of Houston	Tp	
Kilgore College	Tc	Sc
Lamar University, Beaumont	Tc	Sc
Letourneau College, Longview	Tc	Sc

TEXAS (continued)

McMurry College, Abilene	Tc	Sc			
Midland College	Tc	Sc			
Our Lady of the Lake University of San Antonio	Tc				
Paris Junior College	Tc	Sc			
Rice University, Houston	Tp				
Saint Mary's University, San Antonio	Tp				
Schreiner College, Kerrville	Tc	Sp			
Southern Methodist University, Dallas	Tc	Sc			
Tarrant County Junior College, Fort Worth	Tc	Sc			
University of Texas (UT)					
UT at Arlington	Tc				
UT at Austin	P	G	Tc	Sc	F
UT at Dallas	Tp	Sp			
UT at Tyler	Tc	Sc			
Texas A & M University System, College Section	Tc	Sc			
Texas Christian University, Fort Worth	Tp				
Texas Lutheran College, Seguin	Tc	Sc			
Texas Tech University, Lubbock	Tc	Sc			
Texas Wesleyan College, Fort Worth	Tc	Sp			
Trinity College, San Antonio	Tc	Sc			
Victoria College	Tc	Sc			
Western Texas College, Snyder	Tc	Sc			

UTAH

Brigham Young University, Provo	Tc	Sc	F
University of Utah, Salt Lake City	Tp		

VERMONT

Middlebury College	Tp			
Saint Michael's College, Winooski	Tp			
University of Vermont, Burlington	Tp			

VIRGINIA

Hollins Colege, Roanoke	Tp			
Old Dominion University, Norfold	Tp			
University of Richmond	Tp			
Sweet Briar College	Tp			
Virginia Commonwealth University, Richmond	Tc	Sc		
University of Virginia, Charlottesville	Tc	Sc	F	B
University of Virginia-Mary Washington College, Fredericksburg	Tp			
Washington and Lee University, Lexington	Tp			
College of William and Mary, Williamsburg	Tp	Sp		

WASHINGTON

Columbia Basin College, Tri-Cities	Tc	Sc			
Eastern Washington University, Cheney	Tc	F			
Highline Community College, Midway	Tc	Sc	F		
University of Puget Sound, Tacoma	Tc	Sc	F		
Seattle University	Tc				
Seattle Central Community College	Tc				
Seattle Pacific College	Tc				
University of Washington, Seattle	P	Tc	Sp	F	B
Washington State University, Pullman	Tp				
Western Washington University, Bellingham	Tc	F			
Whitman College, Walla Walla	Tc				
Whitworth College, Spokane	Tc				

WEST VIRGINIA

Appalachian Bible College, Bradley	Tc	Sc	F
Bethany College	Tp		
Marshall University, Huntington	Tc	Sp	
Morris Harvey College, Charleston	Tp		
West Virginia University, Morgantown	Tc	Sc	
West Virginia Wesleyan College, Buckamoon	Tp	Sp	F
Wheeling College	Tc	Sc	F

WISCONSIN

Beloit College	Tp				
Cardinal Stritch College, Milwaukee	Tp				
Marquette University, Milwaukee	Tp				

University of Wisconsin

Madison Campus	D	G	Tc	Sc	F	B
Milwaukee Campus	P	G	Tp	Sp		
Superior Campus	Tp					

WYOMING

Casper College	Tp	Sp
Central Wyoming College, Riverton	Tp	Sp
Laramie County College	Tp	Sp
Northwest Community College, Powell	Tp	Sp
University of Wyoming, Laramie	Tp	Sp
Western Wyoming College, Rock Springs	Tp	Sp

URUGUAY

Universidad de la República, Montevideo   Tc   F

VENEZUELA

Universidad Central de Venezuela, Caracas   Tp   Sp   F

YUGOSLAVIA

Univerzitet u Sarajevu   Tp   F

PART TWO

Syllabi

SYLLABI

The listing includes:

- courses regularly given in universities, but not those given in Jewish seminaries, teacher training colleges or Israeli institutions
- courses given by visiting faculty on a temporary basis (marked *)
- courses in which there is some significant Jewish content (marked **)
- courses for which the World Register does not have the instructor's name (These are listed alphabetically by institution in appendix)

The years given in brackets indicate the dates listed on the syllabi.

Following the list of syllabi will be found a subject index cross-referenced with the syllabi according to author.

ABLIN, Mario and   Universidad de Chile, Chile
Pinhas Avivi   Introducción a la Sociología Judía I, II [1978]

ALBERTSON, R.G.   University of Puget Sound, USA
                           **Religion and Literature

ALEXANDER, Edward   University of Washington at Seattle, USA
                           Literature of the Holocaust

ANDERSON, John C.   Bryan College, USA
                           Elementary Hebrew

ANDERSON, Daniel L.   Appalachian Bible College, USA
                           Pentateuch Syllabus [1982]

ANGRESS, Ruth   Princeton University, USA
                           Literature of the Holocaust [1983]

ANKORI, Zvi   University of Texas at Dallas, USA
                           Jewish Historians and Ideas of Jewish History [1984]
                           The Jewish Historical Experience: Jewry and Judaism
                             under Judaism under Medieval Christendom [1984]
                           Messianism and Sectarian Movements in Medieval
                             Jewry [1985]
                           Topics in Middle Eastern History: Jews and Judaism in
                             the Orbit of Islam [1985]

ARANOV, Saul   University of Natal, South Africa
                           Diaspora Judaism and Religious Encounters [1984]

49

ARANOV (cont'd)   Institutions, Issues and Ideas in Contemporary
                                    Judaism [1984]

                                 Judaism During the Second Commonwealth [1984]

...... and Rachel   Judaism and the Jewish People [1982]
Puterman

ASKENAZI, Joel   Institut Martin Buber, Belgium

                                 La Signification Religieuse et Philosophique du
                                    Mouvement Hassidique [1975-76]

AUERBACH, Jerold   Wellesley College, USA

                                 American Jewish History [1984]

                                 The United States and Israel [1987]

AUSTER, Henry   University of Toronto, Canada

                                 Jewish Fiction in North America [1984]

AVERY-PECK, Alan   Tulane University, USA

                                 American Judaism [1982-83]

                                 Hebrew Prose and Poetry II [1983]

                                 Introduction to Hebrew [1983]

                                 Introduction to Judaism [1983]

                                 The Jew as Hellene: Judaism in the Graeco-Roman
                                    Period [1983]

                                 Modern Judaism [1982]

AVNI, Haim   Universidad Iberoamericana, Mexico

                                 *Exilio y Emigración del Pueblo Judío [1983]

                                 Brandeis University, USA

                                 *World Jewry Today: The Contemporary Position of
                                    the Jewish People and its Immediate Historical
                                    Background [1983]

50

BANKIER, David   Universidad Iberoamericana, Mexico
                          *Historia Nacional y Universal del Pueblo Judío:
                          Una Introducción Metodológica [1982]
                          *Del Antisemitismo Moderno al Antisionismo [1985]

BARON, John Herschel   Tulane University, USA
                          Jewish Music

BARTH, Lewis   University of Southern California, USA
                          Survey of Rabbinical Literature [1981]

BARYLKO, Jaime   Universidad de Belgrano, Argentina
                          *Cinco Mil Años de Pensamiento Judío [1984]

BAUMGARTEN, Albert   McMaster University, Canada
                          Introduction to Post-Biblical Judaism

BECK, Norman A.   Texas Lutheran College, USA
                          Anti-Jewish Polemic in the New Testament and the
                          Church Today [1978]

BEN AMI, Shlomo   Universidad Iberoamericana, Mexico
                          *Historia del Estado de Israel [1985]

BEN RAFAEL, Eliezer   Institut Martin Buber, Belgium
                          La Place de L'Intellectuel dans la Société
                          Juive Traditionelle, dans la Diaspora
                          Contemporaine et en Israël [1977-78]

BENSIMON, Doris   Institut Martin Buber, Belgium
                                Problèmes d'Acculturation en Milieu Juif
                                [1972-73]

BERDICHEVSKY, Bernardo   Universidad de Chile, Chile
                                Prehistoria y Orígenes de la Civilización
                                en el Cercano Oriente I, II [1973]

BERGER, Alan   Syracuse University, USA
                                Holocaust [1982]
                                Jewish-Christian Encounter [1983]
                                Jewish Mysticism [1978]
                                Judaism [1981; 1982]
                                Judaism in American Fiction [1978; 1983]
                                Literature and Theology in Post-Holocaust
                                Studies [1982]

BERNER, Leila   Reed College, USA
                                Jewish-Christian Relations in the Middle Ages
                                [1984]
                                Introduction to Judaism [1983-84]
                                Special Topics in Jewish History (I): To the
                                Eighth Century [1983-84]
                                Special Topics in Jewish History (II): Middle
                                Ages and Modern Period [1984]

BIER, Jean Paul   Institut Martin Buber, Belgium
                                Auschwitz et les Nouvelles Littératures
                                Allemandes [1974-75]

BLASI, Joseph   Harvard University, USA
                                Sociology of the Kibbutz

BLUMBERG, Arnold   Towson State University, USA
                         Survey of Jewish History [1982]

BLUMENTHAL, David   Brown University, USA
                            Introduction to Judaism [1975-76]
                            Modern Judaism [1975-76]
                            The Mystical Tradition in Judaism [1975-76]
                            Topics in Modern Jewish History [1975-76]

...... and J. Boozer   Emory University, USA
                            The Holocaust [1977-78]

BOGARD, B.   Black Hills State College, USA Biblical Literature
                            [1984]

BÖHM, Günther   Universidad de Chile, Chile
                            Historia del Judaísmo Latinoamericano [1978]

BOID, R.M.   Victoria College, Australia
                            Medieval Jewish History [1984]
                            Problems of Jewish Philosophy [1984]

BOK, Willy   Institut Martin Buber, Belgium
                            Demographie de la Diaspora de 1900 à nos
                            jours [1972-73]
                            L'entre-Deux-Guerres: Realités et Grandes
                            Courants Idéologiques [1978-79]
                            Le Judaïsme Américain de 1880 à 1914 [1980-81]
                            Le Judaïsme Américain de 1914 à 1945 [1981-82]
                            La Modernisation de la vie Juive en Occident

BONKOVSKY, Fred,   Emory University, USA
J. Boozer and V. Thompson   The Holocaust [1983]

BOONE, Jerome   Lee College, USA
                              Intertestamental Period
                              Old Testament Survey

BORG, Marc   Oregon State University, USA
                              The Old Testament [1981]

BOWMAN, Steven   University of Cincinnati, USA
                              Classic Rabbinic Thought: Pirke Aboth [1981]
                              History of Zionism [1981; 1982]

BRAUN, Vivian   Towson State University, USA
                              Elements of Hebrew I, II [1982]

BROOKS, Roger   University of Notre Dame, USA
                              Introduction to Biblical Hebrew [1984-85]
                              Judaism as a Religion: Judaism or Judaisms?
                              [1984-85]
                              Religious Literature: Judaism [1984-85]

                          Brown University, USA
                              Post-Biblical Hebrew: Readings in Post-
                              Exilic, Mishnaic and Midrashic Hebrew
                              [1981-82]

BROWN, Jewel   Sue Bennett College, USA
                              Historical Approach to Old Testament Faith

BROWN, Michael   York University, Canada
                              The Final Solution: Perspectives on the
                                Holocaust [1983-84]
                              From Alien to Archetype: The North American
                                Jew [1983-84]
                              Greek and Biblical Traditions [1983-84]
                              Modern History of the Jews [1983-84]

BURNETT, Steve   University of Wisconsin at Madison, USA
                              Biblical Texts [1983]

BURSTEIN, Stanley   California State University, Los Angeles, USA
                              **The Near East from Alexander to Cleopatra

BUSCH, Joel and   East Los Angeles College, USA
Phyllis Woodworth   The History of Genocide [1983]

CANNON, Dale   Western Oregon State College
                              **Western Religions [1981]

CANO PEREZ, M.J.   Universidad de Granada, Spain
                              Instituciones del Antiguo Testamento y del
                                Judaísmo [1983]
                              Lengua Hebrea I, II, III
                              Paleografía y Epigrafía Hebreas

CARLTON, Jo Ann   Occidental College, USA
                              Hebrew Life and Literature [1981]
                              Qumran and Apocrypha [1981]

55

CARTER, E.   University of California, Los Angeles, USA
                             **Seminar in Ancient Near Eastern Archaeology:
                                Egypt and Western Asia, 4000-1200 B.C.E. [1982]

CESARANI, D.   Leeds University, UK
                             Modern Jewish History since c. 1700 [1984]

CHALLENER, Richard D.   Princeton University, USA
and Nancy J. Weiss   **The United States: The 1890s to 1941 [1983-84]

CHAZAN, Robert   CUNY-Queens College, USA
                             The Jews in the Medieval Islamic World [1983]
                             History of the Jewish People I [1983]
                             History of the Jewish People II [1983]
                             Studies in Jewish History [1984]

COHEN, Joseph   Tulane University, USA
                             Modern American Jewish Literature [1983]

COHEN, M.R.   Princeton University, USA
                             Early Modern Jewish History to 1789 [1981]
                             The Jews in Medieval Europe [1983]
                             The Jews under Medieval Islam [1982; 1984]

COHEN, Steven   CUNY, Queens College, USA
                             The American Jewish Community [1982]

COHN, Robert L.   Northwestern University, USA
                               The Art of Biblical Narrative
                               History of Judaism [1984]
                               The Legends of Genesis [1981]
                               Old Testament: Its Nature and Content [1981-82]
                               Special Topics: Prophecy
                               Topics in Judaism: Jewish Responses to Catastrophe

...... and Kenneth Seeskin   Ancient Civilization: Israel and Greece [1984]

COLLINS, John J.   Northwestern University, USA
                               Topics in Judaism: Apocalyptic Literature

COMBS, A.E.   McMaster University, Canada
                               The Five Books of Moses

COOPER, Alan   McMaster University, Canada
                               Biblical Interpretation, Traditional and Modern
                               Prophecy in Ancient Israel
                               Religion and Literature in Ancient Israel

CRAIGIE, Peter C.   University of Calgary, Canada
                               Classical Hebrew I, II [1983-84]

CUTRER, Clyde   Appalachian Bible College, USA
                               Introduction to the Bible [1982]

CUTTER, William   University of Southern California, USA
                               Evil, Suffering, Goodness and Hope in the
                               Jewish Experience

57

DAVIDS, Leo

York University, Canada
The Jewish Community [1977-78]
Jewish Communities: Structure, Direction and Problems [1980]

DAVIES, Alan

University of Toronto, Canada
Antisemitism [1977-78]

DAVIS, N.Z., T. Rabb and M. Cohen

Princeton University, USA
The Jews in Europe, 1500-1800

DASH-MOORE, Deborah

Vassar College, USA
Jewish Religion and Ethnicity in America
Religion and Secularism in Modern Jewish Thought [1984]
World Jewry since 1945 [1984]

DASHEFSKY, A.

University of Connecticut, USA
American Jewry [1984]

DEAN MCBRIDE, S.

Brown University, USA
The Restoration Program of Ezekiel 40-48 [1977-78]

DELMAIRE, M.

Université de Lille III, France
Israël 1948-1973

DERCZANSKY, Alex

Institut Martin Buber, Belgium
Les Institutions Communautaires Juives [1975-76]
La Langue Yiddish [1978-79]

DEVENS, Monica

Pomona College, USA

    Hebrew 1a-1b [1982]

    Elementary Modern Hebrew [1982]

    Intermediate Modern Hebrew [1982]

    Advanced Modern Hebrew [1982]

    Readings in Modern Hebrew Language and Literature [1982]

DIAMENT, Carol

CUNY, Queens College, USA

    Judaism and Jewish Women [1984]

DIETRICH, Wendell S.

Brown University, USA

  **Contemporary Religious Thought: Judaic and Christian [1976-77; 1978-79]

  **History of Christian Thought: Nineteenth Century [1981-82]
  **The Myth of the Judeo-Christian Tradition [1981]
  **Religion and Alienation in XXth Century Culture [1978-79]

DOBKOWSKI, Michael

Hobart and William Smith College, USA

    The History and Impact of the Holocaust [1976]

DON, Yehuda

Harvard University, USA

  *The Economic History of the Kibbutz [1980]

DORI, Rivka

University of Southern California, USA

    Hebrew I [1981]

    Hebrew II [1982]

    Hebrew III [1981-82]

    Hebrew IV [1982]

DURNBAUGH, D.F.   Bethany Theological Seminary, USA

                         **Seminar in Modern Church History: The Confessing
                            Church [1976]

ECKARDT, Alice L.   Lehigh University, USA

                         The Holocaust: Its History and Meaning [1978]

EISEN, Arnold   Columbia University, USA

                         Encounters between Modern Philosophy and
                            Judaism [1981]

                         Martin Buber and his Critics [1982]

                         Modern Jewish Civilization [1981]

EISENMAN, Robert   California State University, Long Beach, USA

                         Dead Sea Scrolls

                         History of the Jewish Religion

                         Jewish History

                         Modern Jewish Thought/Zionism

                         Old Testament Literature and Religion/
                            Introduction to the Old Testament

ELIACH, Yaffa   CUNY, Brooklyn College, USA

                         The Literature of the Holocaust [1978]

                         The Period of the Holocaust

ELLENSON, David   University of Southern California, USA

                         Introduction to Judaism [1982]

                         Jewish Ethics [1981]

ENCEL, Sol   University of New South Wales, Australia

                         The Jews in Contemporary Society

60

ENSOR, William   Patten College, USA
                             Ancient Israel
                             Backgrounds to the Old Testament
                             Pentateuch
                             Prophetic Literature (Pre-Exilic)
                             Prophetic Literature II
                             Wisdom Literature

ESLINGER, M.L.   University of Calgary, Canada
                             The Beginnings of Hebrew Religion [1984]

FAGIN, Helen   University of Miami, USA
                             Literature of the Holocaust

FALES, Frederich   Universita degli Studi di Padova, Italy
                             Ebraico e Lingue Semitiche Comparate [1977-78]

FALK, Zeev   Universidade de São Paulo, Brazil
                             *Direito Talmudico [1984]

FASBENDER, Sister Bennet Mount Mary College, USA
                             Our Judaic Heritage [1983]

FEINGOLD, Henry   Bernard Baruch College, USA
                             History of the Jews in America [1976; 1982]

FELDMAN, Louis H.   Yeshiva University, USA
                             The Dialogue of Paganism and Judaism in the
                             Greek and Roman World

FELKIN, Bezalel   Universidad do Estado do Rio de Janeiro, Brazil
                         Lingua Hebraica I, II, III, IV
                         Literatura Hebraica I, II

FELSTINER, John   Stanford University, USA
                         Literature of the Holocaust [1979; 1980; 1981-82;
                         1982-83]

FENTON, Jason   Orange Coast College, USA
                         History of Judaism [1981; 1984]

FERNANDEZ VALLINA,   Universidad Complutense de Madrid, Spain
   Francisco J.   Arameo II

FIELD, E.   University of California, Los Angeles, USA
                         The Jews in the Ancient World

FIERMAN, Morton C.   California State University, Fullerton, USA
                         The Holocaust

FINET, André   Institut Martin Buber, Belgium
                         Rapports entre la Mésopotamie et le Monde Biblique
                         [1974-75]

FORRESTER, Kent   Murray State University, USA
                         The Bible as Literature

FOX, Harry   University of Toronto, Canada
                         Aspects of Early Rabbinic Judaism
                         Judaism and its Hellenistic Environment [1983-84]

FRANCO, Leonard | Pasadena City College, USA
Literature of the Bible I, II [1979-80]

FRERICHS, Ernest S. | Brown University
Biblical Interpretation [1977-78]
**Biblical Interpretation in Judaism and
Christianity [1975-76]
Old Testament Theology [1975-76]

...... and D. Hirsch | Studies in Biblical Literature: Biblical
Narrative [1980-81]
Studies in Biblical Literature: The Book of Job
and Jobian Literature [1975-76; 1977-78]
Studies in Biblical Literature: the Song of
Songs and the Love Lyric [1978-79]

...... and Irving
Mandelbaum | Hebrew Bible Translation [1976-77]

FRIZZELL, Lawrence | Seton Hall University, USA
The Holocaust: History and Theological Issues

GABRIEL, L. | Sacramento City College, USA
Jewish Civilization [1982-84]

63

GARBER, Zeev   Los Angeles Valley College,USA
                              Hebrew Civilization I, II
                              History of the Jewish People [1972]
                              Holocaust: A Prototype of Genocide
                              Israel: The Theory and Practice of Zionism
                              The Jewish Religious Heritage
                              Modern Hebrew Literature in Translation
                              Survey of Jewish Philosophy, Thought and Culture
                              The Talmud: Mishnah as Literature

GARLICK, Antony   Wayne State College, USA
                              **History and Literature of Music

GARRISON, C.   Oregon State University, USA
                              **World Literature

GARSHOWITZ, L.   University of Toronto, Canada
                              The Akedah in Post-Biblical Hebrew Literature
                              The Jewish-Christian Encounter
                              Judaism
                              Medieval Hebrew Prose and Poetry
                              The Rabbinic Mind

GARY, Phillips   Bryan College, USA
                              Poetic Books of the Bible

GERO, Stephen   Brown University, USA
                              **Christianity in Late Antiquity [1976-77]

GERSHENZON, Shoshana   Los Angeles Valley College, USA
         The Holocaust [1981]

GIRON BLANC, Luis   Universidad Complutense de Madrid, Spain
         Lengua Hebrea III
         Textos Hebreos Postbíblicos

GITTLEN, B.   Towson State University, USA
         Interpretations of the Bible: The Old Testament

GLAZER, Nathan   Harvard University, USA
         American Jews [1977]

GOLDSTEIN, Jerrold   Los Angeles Valley College, USA
         The Jew in America

GOLDSTEIN, Judith L.   Vassar College, USA
         Anthropology in Israel [1984]

GOOD, Robert M.   Brown University, USA
         Introduction to the Bible: Ancient Israel [1980–81]
         Israelite Religion in its Near Eastern Context
         [1980–81]
         Religious Myth and Epic of the Ancient Near East
         [1980–81]
         The Response to Exile [1980–81]

GOODBLATT, David   Brown University, USA
         The History of Judaism in the Medieval Period
         [1979–80]
         Zionism [1979–80]

GORDON HARRIS, J.   North American Baptist Seminary, USA
                         Biblical Archaeology [1983]
                         Elementary Hebrew [1983]
                         Hebrew Exegesis [1982; 1983]
                         Nature and Background of Languages of the Bible
                         Prophets and Writings
                         Seminar on Isaiah
                         Seminar on Wisdom Literature [1983]
                         Old Testament History and Literature

GRAEBNER, Norman A.   University of Virginia, USA
                     **Diplomatic History of the United States since 1920
                       [1983]

GREENBERG, Blu   The College of Mount St. Vincent, USA
                         Jewish-Christian Relations

GREENBERG, Gershon   The American University, USA
                         America and the Holocaust [1981]
                         America and the Holy Land [1981]

GREENBERG, Irving   City University of New York, USA
                         The Holocaust

GREENBERG, S.B.   University of Natal, South Africa
                              Jewish Faith [1980]
                              Jewish Laws and Customs [1980]
                              Seminar on Abraham Joshua Heschel
                              Seminar on Hasidism
                              Survey of Jewish History
                              Zionist History and Ideology

GREENSPAHN, F.   University of Denver, USA
                              Archaeology and the Bible [1979]
                              The Bible [1984]
                              Dead Sea Scrolls [1981]
                              The History of Ancient Israel [1982]
                              The History of Israelite Religion [1983]
                              The Holocaust [1984]
                              The Image of Woman in the Bible
                              The Literature of Rabbinic Judaism [1983]
                              Prophets of Israel [1982]
                              Understanding the Old Testament

GRUMET, M.   Brown University, USA
                              Jewish Secular Culture in America, 1906-1965
                                 [1979-80]

GUROCK, Jeffrey S.   Yeshiva University, USA
                              History of the Jews in America
                              The Jewish Religion in America

HALPERIN, David J.   University of North Carolina, USA

                          Introduction to Jewish Civilization [1983]

                          The Messiah and the Apocalypse [1982; 1984]

                          Problems in the New Testament and Rabbinic Judaism [1983]

...... and Gordon Newby   Problems in Rabbinic Judaism and Early Islam [1982]

HALPERIN, Irving   San Francisco State College, USA

                          The American Jewish Writer

HALPERN, Baruch   York University, Canada

                          The Bible and the Ancient Near East [1978-79]

                          Israelite Prophecy

                          Law and Authority in Israel and the Ancient Near East

                          Problems in Israelite Prophecy

HANNI, Philip   Willamette University, USA

                          Modern Jewish Thought: Elie Wiesel and Martin Buber [1978]

HARRIS, Brice   Occidental College, USA

                          **The Middle East [1982]

HEILMAN, Samuel C.   CUNY, Queens College, USA

                          The American Jewish Community [1977; 1978; 1983]

                          Orthodox Judaism in America [1981; 1984]

HELMAN, Amir   Harvard University, USA

                          Economics of Labor-Managed Enterprises and the Kibbutz [1984]

HERMAN, Simon   University of Capetown, South Africa

                             *The Social Psychology of Ethnic Identity: The Case
                                of Jewish Identity [1982]

HERSHKOWITZ, Leo   CUNY, Queens College, USA

                             American Jewish History, 17th-20th Centuries [1978]

HIMMELFARB, Martha   Princeton University, USA

                             The American Jewish Community [1984]

                             Classical Judaism [1982]

                             Judaism in the Graeco-Roman World [1982]

                             Rabbinic Judaism [1983]

                             Religion and Literature of the Old Testament [1983]

                             Religion and Literature of the Old Testament:
                                Wisdom Literature and the Post-Exilic Period
                                [1984]

HODARA, Joseph   Universidad Iberoamericana, Mexico

                             *Estratificación de los Judíos en Diferentes
                                Tipos de Sociedad [1984]

HOFFMANN, Stanley   Harvard University, USA

                             **International Conflict in the Modern World [1982]

HOROWITZ, Maryanne   Occidental College, USA

                             Modern Jewish Cultural History [1980]

HOSOI, Y.T.   Oregon State University, USA

                             **Religions of Mankind [1982]

HUGHES, J. Donald   University of Denver, USA
                           **Ancient Dreams and Dream Interpretation
                           **The Environmental History of the Ancient
                             Mediterranean World

HYMAN, Arthur   Columbia University, USA
                           Medieval Islamic and Jewish Philosophy [1978]

                           University of Californa at San Diego, USA
                           Modern and Contemporary Jewish Religious and
                             Intellectual Movements [1977]

                           Yeshiva University, USA
                           Jewish Ethics [1980]
                           Modern and Contemporary Jewish Thought
                           The Philosophy of Maimonides [1977]
                           Survey of Jewish Philosophy

HYMAN, Paula   Columbia University, USA
                           European Jewry in the 20th Century [1979]
                           Western European Jewry from the French Revolution to
                             the 20th Century [1979]

ISRAELI, Raphael   York University, Canada
                           */**War and Peace in the Middle East [1983-84]

JAFFEE, Martin S.   University of Virginia, USA
                               American Judaism [1981]
                               The Holy Man in the Judaic Tradition
                               Jewish Mystical Tradition [1982]
                               Judaism and Historical Catastrophe [1981]
                               Judaism: Life and Ritual
                               Modern Judaic Imagination: Jewish Fiction in America

JENSEN, I.   Bryan College, USA
                            **Bible Seminar
                            **Inductive Method Applied to the Bible [1984]

JICK, Leon A.   Brandeis University, USA
                               Emergence of the American Jewish Pattern [1984]

JOHNSON, Thomas F.   North American Baptist Seminary, USA
                            **Biblical Hermeneutics [1983]

JOINER, Ronald E.   Warner Pacific College, USA
                            **Devotional Use of the Psalms [1981-82]

JOSPE, Raphael   University of Denver, USA
                               Jewish Law and Lore - Rabbinic Literature in
                                  Translation [1984]
                               Jewish Mysticism [1981]
                               Judaism in American Life [1983]
                               The Land of Israel in History and Theology [1984]
                               Modern Jewish Thought [1981]
                               Topics in Jewish Thought [1984]

KAPLAN, Joseph   Universidad Iberoamericana, Mexico
                           *El Impacto de Sefarad en la Historia Judía [1983]

KASSON, Joseph   University of North Carolina, USA
                           **American Cultural History: Class, Culture, Art,
                              Taste and Leisure in America, 1830-1920 [1982]

KATZ, I.   University of Indiana, Bloomington, USA
                           Proseminar in History: Jews and Judaism in America
                              [1978]

KATZ, Michael   University of Pennsylvania, USA
                           **American Social History [1982]

KATZ, Nathan   William College, USA
                           **Antisemitism, Misogyny and Racism [1982]
                           Contemporary Jewish Thought [1981]

KATZ, Steven T.   Dartmouth College, USA
                           Contemporary Jewish History
                           Judaism in Modern Times [1981]

KEIDAR, Benjamin   Universidad Iberoamericana, Mexico
                           *Los Valores Bíblicos y la Sociedad Judía Moderna
                              [1983]

KELLY, Arthur M.   Warner Pacific College, USA
                           The Bible as Literature I [1981]
                           The Bible as Literature II [1983]

72

KENNET, Moshe   Kutztown State College, USA
                         **History of the Middle East

KIENER, Ronald   Dartmouth College, USA
                         Introduction to Judaism

KILEY, M.   St. Jerome's College, Canada
                         Introduction to Biblical Studies I [1983]

KING, Roger   Oregon State University, USA
                         The Bible as Literature

KLECKY, Samuel   Universidad de Chile, Chile
                         Historia Moderna del Pueblo Judío [1978]

KNOPP, Josephine   Temple University, USA
                         The Road to Hitler: The Holocaust as a World Event

KOCHAN, Lionel   University of Warwick, UK
                         From Palestine to Israel, 1936-1948
                         History of Jews in Europe, 1750-1945
                         Jews in Europe and America, 1500-1750

KOGAN, Barry S.   University of Cincinnati, USA
                         Topics in Jewish Philosophy [1980-1]

KORNBERG, J.   University of Toronto, Canada
                         The Holocaust: The Nazis, Occupied Europe and the
                             Jews [1984-85]
                         Modern History of the Jews [1984-85]

KRANZLER, Gershon   Towson State University, USA
                                         Sociology of the American Jewish Community [1980]

KRAUS, E. Robert   Occidental College, USA
                                         Jewish People, Jewish Thought [1982]

KRAUT, Benny   University of Cincinnati,USA
                                         Book of Job and the Problem of Evil
                                         Denominations in Judaism
                                         Jewish Civilization - Biblical to Medieval Age
                                         Jewish-Christian Encounter
                                         Jewish Civilization - Modern European [1981; 1982]
                                         Studies in the Holocaust
                                         Theology and the Holocaust

KREIMAN, Angel   Universidad de Chile, Chile
                                         Literatura Hebrea Post-Bíblica I, II ([978]

KRONFELD, Chana   Cornell University, USA
                                         Hebrew [1981; 1982]
                                         Advanced Modern Hebrew
                               **Metaphor, Modernism and Cultural Context (in
                                         Hebrew, Yiddish, English and American Poetry)
                                         Modern Hebrew Literature in Translation: Modern
                                         Hebrew Poetry [1981-82]
                                         Modern Hebrew Literature in Translation:
                                         The Modern Hebrew Short Story [1982]

LACOCQUE, Andre and   Chicago Theological Seminary, USA
Clyde Manschrek   The Jewish Experience of Suffering [1972-73]

LANDAU, Lazare

Institut Martin Buber, Belgium

La Crise du Judaïsme Français entre les Deux
Guerres Mondiales [1981-82]

Le Judaïsme aux Temps Modernes [1972-73]

LANGER, Lawrence L.

Yale University, USA

**Images of the Survivor [1979]

Simmons College, USA

**The Literature of Atrocity [1972]

LARY, N.

York University, Canada

**Ideology and Morality [1983-84]

LASKER, Daniel J.

University of Toronto, Canada

Classics of the Jewish Tradition in
Translation [1983]

The Philosophy of Maimonides [1984]

LEE, Humphreys W.

Univesity of Tennessee, USA

Ancient Israelite Religious Traditions

The Rise of Judaism

LEE, Marshall

Pacific University, USA

**Adolf Hitler and the Question of Germany [1977]

......and M. Steele

The Holocaust [1984]

75

LIEBMAN, Charles   Brown University, USA

                                        *Judaism and the Human Experience: Religion and
                                        Nationalism [1982-83]

                                        *Judaism in the State of Israel [1982-83]

LIPSTADT, Deborah   University of Washington, Seattle, USA

                                        The Destruction of European Jewry, 1933-1945

                                    University of California, Los Angeles, USA

                                        American Jewish History

                                        American Jewish History to 1914

                                        Institutions of Jewish Life

                                        Modern Jewish National Movements: The Emergence
                                        of Modern Zionism, 1881-1948 [1982]

LITTELL, Frank and   Temple University, USA
Josephine Knopp
                                        **Seminar: Social Pathology - The Holocaust and the
                                        Church Struggle [1977]

LIWERANT, Judit   Universidad Iberoamericana, Mexico

                                        *Historia del Movimiento Nacional Judío [1984]

LOCKSHIN, Marty   York University, Canada

                                        The Jewish Experience: Symbiosis and Rejection
                                        [1980-81]

                                        Prophetic Literature: Text and Classical
                                        Interpretation [1981]

                                        Rabbinic Judaism: Thought and Institutions

LOMASKY, Loren E.   University of Minnesota, Duluth, USA
                       **The Emergence of Christianity [1980-81]
                          Growth of Religious Ideas: The Hebraic Background
                          [1980]

LOWENSTEIN, Egon   Universidad de Chile, Chile
                          Seminario de Teología Judía [1978]

MABEE, Charles   Marshall University, USA
                       **Approaches to the Bible

MACDONALD, J.   University of Glasgow, UK
                       **Ancient Near Eastern History [1979]
                          Hebrew [1979]

MAIDMAN, Maynard P.   York University, Canada
                       **Ancient Near Eastern History [1983-84]
                          The History of Israel from its Origins in the
                             Settlement to the Babylonian Exile [1982-83]

MAIER, Charles S.   Harvard University, USA
                       **Topics in the Twentieth-Century History: The
                          World War [1982-83]

MARRUS, M.R.   University of Toronto, Canada
                          The Holocaust [1980-81]

MASON, Henry L.   Tulane University, USA
                          The Holocaust System: A Political Analysis [1983]

77

MAZOR, Yair   University of Wisconsin at Madison, USA
                                     Survey of Modern Hebrew Literature [1983]

McCREADY, Wayne   University of Calgary, Canada
                                **The Beginnings of Christianity [1984]
                                **World Religions - Western [1984]

McLOUGHLIN, William G.   Brown University, USA

                                **The History of Religion in America: The
                                      Conflict between Personal Faith and Public
                                      Authority, 1609-1983 [1983]

                                **Social and Intellectual History of the U.S.,
                                      1865-Present [1981]

MEHLMAN, Benjamin   California State University-Northridge, USA
                                **Psychology of Prejudice [1982]

MENDELSON, A.   McMaster University, Canada
                                Introduction to Hellenistic Judaism

MILLER, Glenn   Hamilton College, USA
                                **Seminar in Theology: The Holocaust and Faith
                                [1975-76]

MINERBI, Sergio   Institut Martin Buber, Belgium
                                La Position du Vatican a l'Egard d'Eretz Israël
                                après la Première Guerre Mondiale [1975-76]

MISRAHI, M. Robert   Institut Martin Buber, Belgium

                                **L'Antisemitisme de Karl Marx [1972-73]

MITCHELL, Chris   University of Wisconsin at Madison, USA
                                  Biblical Texts

MOEHRING, Horst

Brown University, USA

Judaism before A.D. 70: Palestinian Judaism [1975-76]

Judaism during the Graeco-Roman Age [1980-81]

**Literature, History and Religion of Earliest Christianity [1975-76]

**Religions of the Hellenistic Age [1975-76]

**History and Historiography - Hellenistic Jewish and Early Christian [1979-80]

**Topics in Early Christianity: The Christian Community and the Roman Empire [1975-76]

Topics in Hellenistic Judaism: Josephus [1976-77]

Topics in Hellenistic Judaism: Judaism before 70 A.D. [1975-76; 1977-78;1979-80]

Topics in Hellenistic Judaism: Philo [1980-81]

**Topics in History of Religions: History of Religions as a Method for the Study of Religions in Antiquity [1978-79]

MORAHG, Gilead

University of Wisconsin at Madison, USA

Biblical Hebrew I [1981]

Biblical Hebrew II [1984]

Hebrew 201, 202 [1983]

Hebrew 301

Israeli Fiction in Translation

Introduction to Hebrew Literature

Survey of Modern Hebrew Literature

MORALDI, L.

Universita di Pavia, Italy

Ebraico e Lingue Semitiche Comparate [1978-79]

MORENO KOCH, Yolanda

Universidad Complutense de Madrid, Spain

Historia de los Judíos Españoles

79

MORLEY, John F.   Seton Hall University, USA
                            The Holocaust: Historical and Religious Aspects
                            of the Nazi Destruction of the Jews [1978]

MORONY, M.   University of California, Los Angeles, USA
                            **Seminar in Medieval Middle Eastern History [1981]

MOSCATI, Gabriella   Istituto Universitario Orientale, Italy
                            Modern Jewish Literature
                            Survey Course on Modern Jewish History and Thought

MOSSE, George   University of Wisconsin at Madison, USA
                            Jewish History in the 19th and 20th Centuries [1976]

MYERS, Philip   Bellevue College, USA
                            **The Second World War

...... and John   **Ancient History
Spivack   **History of Western Civilization I

NADELL, Pamela   American University, USA
                            The American Jewish Community [1984]
                            From Shtetl to Suburbia: American Jewish
                            Literature [1983]

NAHIR, Moshe   University of Manitoba, Canada
                Elementary Hebrew [1983-84]
                Intermediate Hebrew [1983-84]
                Advanced Hebrew [1983-84]
                Hebrew Communication Arts [1983-84]

NAHON, Gerard   Institut Martin Buber, Belgium
                Amsterdam: La Communauté Judeo-Portugaise du
                    XVIIIe. Siècle [1977-78]
                La Diaspora Séfarade du XVIe. au XVIIe. Siècle
                    [1973-74]
                Les Communautés Pionnières du Nouveau Monde
                    [1974-75]
                Communautés Séfarades Contemporaines [1975-76]
                Histoire du Judaïsme Français des Origines à la
                    Révolution [1972-73]
                Le Judaïsme Face à la Chretienté et à
                    l'Islam I: 1497-1776 [1980-81]
                Le Judaïsme Face à la Chretienté et à
                    l'Islam II: XVIIIe.-XIXe. Siècles [1981-82]
                Voie et Problématique de l'Émancipation:
                    Le Modèle Français (1788-1818) [1976-77]

                Université Paris III, France
                Histoire et Civilisation du Judaïsme Séfarade I:
                    L'Essor Médiéval en Afrique du Nord et en
                    Espagne
                Histoire et Civilisation du Judaïsme Séfarade II:
                    La Diaspora Séfarade, XVIe.-XVIIe. Siècles
                Recherches sur les Communautés Séfarades
                    Contemporaines

NAVARRO PEIRO, Angeles   Universidad Complutense de Madrid, Spain
Lengua Hebrea II
Literatura Hebrea Post-Bíblica
Textos Bíblicos

NEAR, Henry   Harvard University, USA
Graduate Seminar: The Kibbutz

NEUSNER, Jacob   Brown University, USA
American Judaism [1975-76; 1984-85]
The Formation of Early Rabbinic Judaism [1977-78]
How To Read a Jewish Book [1975-76]
The Idea of History in Judaism
Introduction to Judaism [1975-76; 1978-79]
Judaism as a Religion [1983-84]
Judaism in Late Antiquity [1976-77; 1980-81]
Talmud Series [1981-82]
Zionism [1975-76; 1978-79]

...... and M. Flesher   American Judaism [1984-85]

...... and Martin Jaffee   Introduction to Judaism [1978-79]

......, Alan Peck and   Law and Society in America [1979-80]
Leonard Gordon

NEWMAN, Aubrey N.   University of Leicester, UK
Europe and the Jewish Problem, 1648-1948 [1983]

NEWMAN, Louis

Carleton College, USA
American Judaism [1984]
Introduction to Biblical Hebrew [1981-82]
Introduction to Rabbinic Literature [1984]
Modern Judaism [1983]
Zionism and Judaism [1984]

NORICH, Anita

University of Michigan, USA
Literature and the Holocaust

NOVAK, Maximilian E.

University of California, Los Angeles, USA
Jewish American Fiction [1982]

NUSSBAUM, Aaron

York University, Canada
Major Sects and Movements in Jewish History

OLSHEN, B.N.

York University, Canada
The Bible [1983-84]

OPPENHEIM, Samuel

California State University-Stanislaus, USA
The Holocaust [1983]
Judaism and Jewish History [1983]

ORBACH, Alexander

University of Pittsburgh, USA
Jewish Responses to Modernity
History of the Holocaust

ORBACH, William

University of Louisville, USA
    Holocaust
    Judaism and Western Civilization
    Modern Jewish Thought
    The Old Testament
    Survey of Jewish Thought and Culture

ORR, William M.

Warner Pacific College, USA
    **World Religions [1981]

PALTIEL, E.

Victoria College, Australia
    Ancient Jewish History [1984]
    Intellectual History of the Jews [1984]

PARVIN, Earl

Appalachian Bible College, USA
    Old Testament Poetry [1983]

PASSAMANECK, S.M.

University of Southern California, USA
    Foundations of Jewish Law [1982]

PASSELECQ, R.P. Georges

Institut Martin Buber, Belgium
    Abraham Joshua Heschel: Une Interprétation du
    Judaïsme [1977-78]

PATTERSON, Davis
and Manfred Vogel

Northwestern University, USA
    Seminar: Modern Tendencies in the Religions--
    Awareness of Self in Modern Hebrew Fiction

PECK, Alan   Brown University, USA
                                        Introduction to Biblical Hebrew I, II [1980-81]

PELLI, M.   Cornell University, USA
                                        Themes in Modern Hebrew Literature: The
                                        Holocaust [1977]

PENNACCHIETTI, Fabrizio   Università degli Studi di Venezia-Ca'foscari, Italy
and E. Trevisan Semi   Lingua e Letteratura Ebraica [1978-79]

PERAL TORRES, Antonio   Universidad Complutense de Madrid, Spain
                                        Lengua Aramea I

PEREZ CASTRO, Federico   Universidad Complutense de Madrid, Spain
                                        Lengua Hebrea Postbíblica
                                        Literatura del Antiguo Testamento [1984]

PFEFFERKORN, M.   Brown University, USA
                                        The Holocaust Vision in Literature [1980-81]

PINKUS, Benjamin   Institut Martin Buber, Belgium
                                        La Communauté Juive en Russie et en U.R.S.S.
                                        [1977-78]

PLANER, John A.   Manchester College, USA
                                        The Jewish Faith, Culture and People [1981-82]

PORTER, Jack Nusan   Emerson College, USA
                                        History of the Jews [1976]

85

PORTER (cont'd)   Boston University, USA
                            Love, Sex and the Jewish Family

                       Lowell University, USA
                            Principles of Jewish Theology
                            The Sociology of American Jewry
                       **The Sociology of Genocide [1979]

PORTON, Gary G.   University of Illinois, Urbana-Champaign, USA
                            American Judaism [1981]
                       **The Holocaust: Religious Responses [1982]
                            Jewish Practices: A Religio-Historical Approach
                            [1981]
                            Judaism: An Introduction [1982]

PREAUX, Claire   Institut Martin Buber, Belgium
                            Les Juifs dans le Monde Héllénistique [1976-77]

PUTERMAN, Rachel   University of Natal, South Africa
                            Varieties of Jewish Thought and Experience [1984]

RABI, Wladimir   Institut Martin Buber, Belgium
                            La Société Juive en France de 1945 à nos jours
                            [1975-76]

RAMER, Samuel Carroll   Tulane University, USA
                            History of the Jews in Russia: 1772-Present

RAPHAEL, Marc L.   Brown University, USA

                              Judaism and the Human Experience: The Holocaust
                                 [1980-1]

                              Modern Judaism [1980-81]

                              Zionism [1980]

RAPHAEL, Freddy   Institut Martin Buber, Belgium

                              La Spécificité du Judaïsme Antique selon Max
                                 Weber [1976-77]

RASSEKH, Nostratollah   Lewis and Clark College, USA

                              **Middle East in Modern Times [1982]

                              **History of the Middle East from the Rise of
                                 Islam to the Fall of the Ottoman Empire

RAVVEN, Heidi M.   Hamilton College, USA

                              American Judaism [1983]

                              Jewish Thought from the Hellenistic Age to the
                                 Modern Era: Reason and Imagination in Jewish
                                 Religious Expression [1983]

                              Martin Buber [1984]

                              Modern Jewish Thought [1984]

REEDER, John P.   Brown University, USA

                              **Religion and Morality [1975-76]

...... and Martin Jaffee   **Approaches to the Study of Religion [1978-79]

...... and R.S. Sarason   Ethics of Judaism [1977-78]

REEVES, George   Santa Monica College, USA

                              The Literature of the Bible: Old Testament
                                 [1982]

87

RENN, W.   Wheeling College, USA
                           **The Nazi Era and the Holocaust [1983]

REYNOLDS, Stephen C.   University of Oregon, USA
                           **Great Religions [1981]
                             Judaism and Christianity [1976]

RIPPIN, A.   University of Calgary, Canada
                             Judaism in the Modern World [1983]

RISCHIN, Moses   San Francisco State University, USA
                           **Ethnic and Race Relations in the U.S. in the
                             Last Century [1983]
                           **Immigrant and Minority Groups in American
                             History [1973]
                           **Uprooted Americans [1982]

ROBINSON, Ira   Concordia University, Canada
                             The Hebrew Bible [1979]
                             The Jews and Judaism in the Middle Ages [1979]
                             Medieval Jewish Messianism: Myth vs. Metaphysics
                             [1980]
                             Modern Jewish Thought and Institutions to 1880
                             [1979]

ROSE, Neal   University of Manitoba, Canada

         Disputation and Dialogue (Jesus in Jewish Literature) [1983]

         Introduction to Rabbinic Literature

         Jewish Mysticism

         Marriage, Family and Sexuality in Jewish Life [1984]

         Social and Cultural Patterns in Jewish Life

         Voices from the Holocaust [1983]

Rosen, Haïm   Institut Martin Buber, Belgium

         Introduction a L'Étude Linguistique de L'Hébreu Contemporain [1981-82]

         Le Développement du Vocabulaire de L'Hébreu Vivant. Aperçu Historique et Esquisse des Rapports Internes et des Développements au Cours du XXe. Siècle [1973-74]

ROSENBERG, Shalom   Universidad Iberoamericana, Mexico

         *Eslabones Históricos del Judaísmo: Del Mundo Pagano a las Filosofías Modernas [1982]

ROSENFELD, Alvin   University of Indiana, Bloomington, USA

         Literature of the Holocaust

ROSENTHAL, Richard   University of Puget Sound, USA

         History and Literature of Ancient Israel

         Jewish Existence

         Judaism in America

         Law and Judaism

ROTH, Norman and Kenneth Sacks

University of Wisconsin at Madison, USA
>Jews, Greeks and Romans: The Conflict of Civilizations [1981-82]

RUBIATO DIAZ, María Teresa

Universidad Complutense de Madrid, Spain
>Arquelogía Bíblica y Cristiana
>Historia de Israel: El Mundo Bíblico

RUETHER, Rosemary

Harvard Divinity School, USA
>**Christology and the **Adversos Judaeos** Tradition [1973]

Garret Evangelical Theological Seminary, USA
>The Holocaust and the State of Israel [1977]

RYAN, Michael

Drew University, USA
>Death Camp Theology [1974-75]
>Holocaust Studies [1976-77]

SABAR, Yona

University of California, Los Angeles, USA
>A Comparative Study of the Verb in Biblical, Mishnaic and Israeli Hebrew
>Survey of Hebrew Grammar

SAENZ BADILLOS, Angel

Universidad de Granada, Spain
>Hebreo, Primer Curso
>Lengua Hebrea II
>Literatura Hebrea II
>Literatura Hebrea Moderna y Contemporánea

SANCHEZ, Gilberto   Universidad de Chile, Chile
                           Introducción a la Lingüística Semita [1978]

SANDERS, J.T.   University of Oregon, USA
                           **Ancient Near Eastern Religions
                           **Great Religions of the World III

SARASON, Richard   Brown University, USA
                           American Judaism [1976-77]
                           Biblical and Post-Biblical Hebrew: Reading in
                             Biblical Hebrew Poetry and Introduction to
                             Mishnaic Hebrew [1976-77]
                           How to Read a Jewish Book [1976-77]
                           Introduction to Biblical Hebrew [1975-76]
                           Jewish Thought in Modern Times: Reform Judaism
                             and Zionism; Messianism in Modern Judaism
                             [1976-77]
                           Modern Judaism [1978-79]
                           The Modern Study of Midrash [1977-78]
                           Readings in Biblical Hebrew Prose Texts
                             [1975-76]

SCHERR, Lilly   Institut Martin Buber, Belgium
                           L'Antisémitisme Contemporain, de l'Affaire
                             Dreyfus à la Rumeur D'Orléans [1973-74]

SCHNEEBAL PERELMAN, Sophie   Institut Martin Buber, Belgium
                           **Thèmes Bibliques dans l'Art et en Particulier
                             dans la Tapisserie Flamande [1976-77]

SCHOENFELD, Stuart   York University, Canada
                           Jewish Identity in the Modern World [1983-84]

SCHOLNIK, Myron I.   Towson State University, USA
                           The Holocaust [1982]

SCHOVILLE, Keith N.   University of Wisconsin at Madison, USA
                           A Survey of Hebrew Literature

SCULT, Mel   CUNY-Brooklyn College, USA
                           The Holocaust

SEIDLER-FELLER, Chaim   University of California, Los Angeles, USA
                           Jewish Practice and Institutions [1981]

SEPHIHA, Haïm Vidal   Institut Martin Buber, Belgium
                           Judéo-Espagnol: Linguistique et Littérature
                             [1972-73]
                           La Judéo-Hispanité au XIXe. Siècle [1976-77]
                           Langue et Littérature Judéo-Espagnoles [1974-75]
                           Presentation Générale de la Littérature
                             Judéo-Espagnole [1975-76]

SERPER, Arie   Insitut Martin Buber, Belgium
                           Les Juifs en Occitanie au Moyen Age [1977-78]

SHAIN, Milton   University of Cape Town, South Africa
                           South African Jewry in the Context of Modern
                             Jewish History

SHAPIRO, Michel   University of Illinois, Urbana-Champaign, USA
                           Jewish Experience in Literature: American Jewish
                             Writers [1981; 1982; 1983]

SHATZMILLER, J.   University of Toronto, Canada
                           Medieval Jewish History [1983-84]

SHENHAR, Shlomo   University of Cape Town, South Africa
                                       Introduction to the Jewish History of the Middle
                                       Ages, 632-1668 [1982]

SHISHIDO, Miles M.   Pacific University, USA
                                     **Religions of the World [1981-82]
                                       Understanding the Old Testament [1970]

SHIVELY, Fredrick H.   Warner Pacific College, USA
                                       The Literature of the Old Testament [1981]

...... and Milo Chapman   Old Testament Exegesis: Proverbs [1981]

SHMIDMAN, Michael A.   University of Cincinnati, USA
                                       History of the Jews in the Medieval Period
                                       Introduction to Jewish Civilization-Medieval
                                       Introduction to Jewish Civilization
                                       Introduction to the Talmud
                                       Judaism and Modern Ethical Problems
                                       Law and Spirituality in Judaism
                                       Messianism in Judaism

SIGNER, Michael A.   University of Southern California, USA
                                       Introduction to Jewish History

SIRAT, M. René   Institut Martin Buber, Belgium
                                       Introduction à l'Historie de la Littérature
                                       Hébraïque [1972-73]

SLAVIN, A.J.   University of Louisville, USA
                                       The Holocaust: The Events and the Western
                                       Imagination [1980]

SOJCHER, M. Jacques

Institut Martin Buber, Belgium

Le Judaïsme et les Juifs dans la Philosophie de Nietzsche [1972-73]

SORENSON, Lloyd

University of Oregon, USA

**World Civilizations [1980]

SOTOODEH KAR, Mohammed

University of Southern California, USA

**Politics of North Africa and the Middle East [1982]

SPATZ, Erwin

Institut Martin Buber, Belgium

Les Juifs dans l'Oeuvre des Principaux Romanciers Français de la Génération de l'Affaire Dreyfus [1976-77]

STEIN, George H.

State University of New York, Binghamton, USA

**Hitler's Europe: The Rise and Fall of the Third Reich [1976]

STEINBERG, Lucien

Institut Martin Buber, Belgium

La Résistance Juive dans l'Europe Occupée [1975-76

STERN, M.S.

University of Manitoba, Canada

Introduction to Judaism II [1984]

Jewish Ethics [1982]

Jewish History [1981-82]

Jews in and of the Arab Lands [1984]

STERN, Stephen

University of Califorma, Los Angeles, USA

Introduction to Jewish Folklore [1982-83]

94

STEUER, Axel D.   Occidental College, USA
                                **Religion in Modern Culture [1982]

STIEGLITZ, R.R.   Rutgers University, USA
                                    Biblical Text: Hebrew
                                    Jewish History to the Roman Period
                                    Jewish History: Medieval and Modern

STILLMAN, Norman   State University of New York, Binghamton, USA
                                    Medieval Jewish History [1983]
                                    Mideast Jews in Modern Times [1984]
                                    Modern Jewish History [1981]

...... and M. Sullivan   Jews and Arabs: A Comparative History [1981]

STITES, Del   Bellevue College, USA
                                **Dying and Death
                                **Religions of the West

STRUS, Andrzej   Università Pontificia Salesiana, Italy
                                    Lingua Ebraica I, II [1978-79]

SZAFRAN, M. Willy   Institut Martin Buber, Belgium
                                    Psychanalyse et Judaïsme [1972-73]

TALMAGE, Frank   University of Toronto, Canada
                                    Jewish Mysticism and Messianism [1977-78]

TANENZAPF, Sol

York University, Canada

The Development of Jewish Thought and Literature [1983]

History of Jewish Thought

Introduction to Jewish Philosophy [1982-83]

Problems in the Study of Judaism: Ritual and Ethics [1983-84]

TAYLOR, Jerome

University of Wisconsin at Madison, USA

**Biblical and Classical Sources of Middle Ages English Literature [1982-83]

THOMPSON, Vivian

Emory University, USA

Jewish Experience in 20th Century Art

......, Fred Bonkovsky and Jack Boozer

The Holocaust [1983]

TIEFEL, Hans

College of William and Mary, USA

Topics in Contemporary Religion: The Holocaust [1976]

TIGAY, Jeffrey H.

University of Pennsylvania, USA

The Bible as Literature [1984]

The History and Civilization of Israel in the Biblical Period

The History of the Religion of Ancient Israel [1984]

Introduction to the Study of Jewish Literature

TORRES FERNANDEZ, Antonio

Universidad de Granada, Spain

Arameo

Literatura Hebrea I: Literatura Bíblica

TRIBLE, Phyllis   Brown University, USA
                                        Introduction to the Bible: Ancient Israel [1978-79]

TULLOCK, John H.   Appalachian Bible College, USA
                                        Old Testament Prophets

TURNIANSKY, Java   Universidad Iberoamericana, Mexico
                                        *La Cultura Ashkenazí y su Vigencia en la Vida
                                            Judía [1983]

TWISS, Sumner B.   Brown University, USA
                                        **Approaches to the Study of Religion [1975-76]
                                        **Comparative Religious Ethics [1980-81]

...... and R. Sarason   **History and Hermeneutics [1976-77]

...... and E. Frerichs   **Theory of Religion [1980-81]

...... and David Little   */**Comparative Religious Ethics [1980]

UMANSKY, Ellen   Emory University, USA
                                        The Ethics of Judaism [1983]
                                        Introduction to Judaism [1983]
                                        The Modernization of Judaism [1983]
                                        Special Topics in Religion: Women in Judaism
                                            [1983]
                                        Special Topics in Religion: Zionism [1984]

UNGER, Leopold   Institut Martin Buber, Belgium
                                        Les Communautés Juives dans les Pays de l'Est:
                                            Problème des Juifs en Union Soviétique
                                            [1972-73]

97

VAN BUREN, Paul

Temple University, USA
    Christianity and Judaism

VAN PUFFELEN, John

Appalachian Bible College, USA
    Old Testament Prophetic Books [1982]

VAUGHAM, Gilbert

Wayne State College, USA
    Literature of the Bible [1983]

VEENKER, Ronald

Western Kentucky University, USA
    Judaism [1978]

VEGAS MONTANER, Luis

Universidad Complutense de Madrid, Spain
    Hebreo IV
    Lengua Hebrea I

VERBIT, Mervin F.

CUNY, Brooklyn College, USA
    Sociology of the American Jewish Community

VOGEL, Manfred H.

Northwestern University, USA
    Introduction to Judaism [1984-85]
    Judaism in Contemporary Christian Theology
    Modern Jewish Thought
    Theology of the Rabbis
    Topics in Judaism: Thought of Martin Buber
    The Understanding of Christianity in Modern
      Jewish Thought

WALDEN, Daniel

Pennsylvania State University, USA

The Yiddish Root and the American Stem [1974]

WALLER, Harold

McGill University, Canada

The Canadian Jewish Community and the Jewish Political Tradition

WALLER, Herbert and
Matthias Neuman

Saint Meinrad College, USA

Jewish Studies [1984]

WASSERMAN, Mordechai

York University, Canada

Hebrew III [1983-4]

WEILL, Georges

Institut Martin Buber, Belgium

Une Communauté Juive à l'Époque de l'Émancipation: l'Example de l'Alsace [1978-79]

L'Émancipation des Juifs [1978-79]

Introduction à la Recherche en Histoire Juive [1976-77]

Les Juifs et la Société Européenne, du Siècle des Lumières à l'Affaire Dreyfus [1979-80]

WEINBERG, David

University of Michigan, USA

Modern Jewish History, 1700-1880 [1984]

Modern Jewish History, 1880-Present [1983]

WEINFELD, Morton

McGill University, Canada

Sociology of the Jews in North America [1982]

WEISS, A.   University of Natal, South Africa
                                 Intellectual Jewish History
                                 Jewish Ethics and Mysticism

WEISSBACH, Lee Shai   University of Louisville, USA
                                 History of the Jews in Modern Times [1980]

WEISSLER, Chava   Princeton University, USA
                                 Jewish Folklore [1984]
                                 Modern Judaism [1983]

WERNER, Rita R.   Los Angeles Valley College, USA
                                 The Bible as Literature [1982]

WILLIAMS, Peter W.   University of Miami, USA
                                 The Jewish Religion and People in America [1984]
                                 Judaism as a Religion [1984]

WILLIAMS, Walter   University of Cincinnati, USA
                                 **Sexual Variance in History [1980]

WINKLER, Alan   Bryan College, USA
                                 Old Testament Survey
                                 **Prophecy and the End of Times
                                 Prophetic Books Syllabus

WOODWORTH, Phyllis and   East Los Angeles College, USA
Joel Busch   The History of Genocide [1983]

WYLEN, Stephen   Marshall University, USA
                                 The Jewish Experience [1983]

YONKER, Nicholas J.   Oregon State University, USA
                                 **Introduction to the World's Religions [1982]

ZAHAVY, T.   Brown University, USA
                                 Modern Hebrew Literature Studies: The Short
                                    Story [1975-76]

ZAIMAN, Joel H.   Brown University, USA
                                 Talmud Series [1975-76]

ZENNER, Walter   State University of New York, Albany, USA
                                 American Jewish Cultures [1981]

ZIPPERSTEIN, Steve   Oxford University, UK
                                 Anglo-Jewish History, 1656-1956
                                 Assimilation and Late 19th-, Early 20th-Century
                                    Jewish History [1984]
                                 The Jewish Experience in Europe, 1848-1948
                                    [1983]

ZUCKERMAN, Alan   Brown University, USA
                                 **Revolution and Counterrevolution [1981]
                                 Strategies of Survival: Jewish Society and
                                    Politics during the Last Century [1980]

...... and Calvin   Strategies of Survival: Jewish Society and
Goldscheider   Politics during the Last Century [1978]

101

ZUCKERMAN, Marvin S.   Los Angeles Valley College, USA
                                 American-Jewish Literature [1974]
                                 College Yiddish I, II [1982]
                                 Yiddish Literature in English Translation [1977]

ZÚÑIGA, Jorge   Universidad de Chile, Chile
                                 Historia Lingüística de los Judíos [1973]

ZYGIELBAUM, A.   University of Southern California, USA
                                 Hasidic Literature [1981]
                                 Holocaust [1982]
                                 Holocaust Literature [1976]
                                 Yiddish Language and Literature

APPENDIX

University of California, Los Angeles, USA	Hebrew Literature in English
University of Cape Town, South Africa	Hebrew I, II, III [1983] Hebrew Culture I, II [1981-82] Jewish Religion I, II [1984] Religious and Biblical Studies I, II, III
Universidad de Chile, Chile	Gramática del Idioma Hebreo I, II, III, IV, V, VI [1978] Historia Contemporánea del Pueblo Judío [1978] Historia de la Cultura Judía I, II [1978] Historia Hebrea Bíblica I, II [1978] Historia Judía Post-Bíblica I, II [1983] Historia Judía Medieval [1978] Introducción a la Filosofía Judía I, II [1978] Literatura Hebrea Bíblica I, II [1978]
University of Cincinnati, USA	Jews in Palestine to 1800 Modern Israel [1980]

Universidad de Granada, Spain	Hebreo Moderno
	Historia de Israel
	Historia de los Judíos en la Edad Media [1983]
	Historia del Texto Bíblico y sus Versiones e Introducción a la Crítica Textual
	Introducción a la Lingüítica Semítica
	Israel Moderno y Contemporáneo
	Judaística: Introducción Metodológica
	Lengua y Literatura Sefaradí [1979]
	Paleografía Hebrea
	Primeros Poetas Hispanohebreos
Los Angeles Valley College, USA	Hebrew I [1982]
McGill University, Canada	Interdisciplinary Lectures in Jewish Studies [1975]
University of Natal, South Africa	Bible and Hebrew Literature
	Jewish Biblical Studies
	Jewish Laws and Customs
	Post-Biblical Jewish Literature
University of Notre Dame, USA	Judaism in Late Antiquity
Oregon State University, USA	**World Literature

Prahran College of Advanced Education, Australia	The Development of Modern Jewish Education [1980]
	Intellectual History of the Jews
	Jewish History and Civilization I: Ancient Period [1979]
	Jewish History and Civilization II: The Middle Ages [1979]
	Jewish History and Civilization III: Emancipation to Present [1979]
	Modern Jewish Literature in English [1979]
	Problems of Jewish Philosophy [1979]
	Sociology and Demography of Jewry [1979]
	Yiddish I, II, III [1979]
Purdue University, USA	Introduction of Jewish Studies [1983]
University of Regina, Canada	Introduction to Judaism
Rhodes University, South Africa	Biblical Studies [1979]
Universidade de São Paulo, Brazil	Cultura Judaica I, II [1983]
	Cultura do Povo Judeu na Antiguidade I,II [1983]
	Cultura do Povo Judeu no Idade Média I, II [1983]
	Cultura do Povo Judeu nos Tempos Modernos I, II [1983]
	Leitura de Texto Hebraicos I, II [1983]
	Língua Hebraica I, II, III, IV, V, VI, VII, VIII [1983]
	Literatura Hebraica I, II, III, IV, V, VI, VII, VII [1983]
	Literatura Hebraica Clássica I, II [1983]
	Literature Hebraica Moderna I, II [1983]

University of Toronto, Canada	History of the Jews in Spain and Portugal until 1391
	History of the Marranos and the Inquisition
	The Jews in the Greco-Roman Period
	Introduction to Jewish Civilization
	Newspaper Hebrew
Victoria College, Australia	Modern Jewish History [1984]
Wabash College, USA	**Cultures and Traditions [1984]
	History and Literature of the Old Testament [1984]
West Virginia Wesleyan College, USA	Introduction to the Bible [1982-3]
	Old Testament Studies I [1980-1]
University of Wisconsin at Madison, USA	Biblical Archaelogy
	Biblical Archaelogy: Proseminar on the Discoveries at Ras Shamra, Qumran and Tell Mardikh
	Elements of Aramaic
	Hebrew
	Jewish Civilization in Medieval Spain
	Jewish Cultural History
	Medieval-Modern Hebrew Literature
University of Washington in Seattle, USA	Contemporary Jewish Problems
York University, Canada	**Hagiographical Literature: Text and Classical Interpretation
	Selected Fragments from the First Prophets [1984]

THEMATIC INDEX OF SYLLABI

I. **Archaeology and Related Studies**

II. **Art**

III. **Bible**

> 1) Studies in the Hebrew Bible; 2) History of the Biblical Text; 3) Bible as Literature.

IV. **Contemporary Jewry**

V. **History**

> 1) General Survey; 2) Ancient History; 3) Medieval History; 4) Modern and Contemporary History; 5) Local History; 6) Special Topics.

VI. **Holocaust Studies**

> 1) Historical, Social and Religious Studies; 2) Literature.

VII. **Judaism and Jewish Thought**

> 1) General Survey; 2) Religion; 3) Ancient Judaism; 4) Rabbinic and Medieval Judaism; 5) Modern and Contemporary Judaism; 6) Mysticism; 7) Ethics; 8) Judaism and Christianity; 9) Other Special Topics.

VIII. **Language - Hebrew**

> 1) General and Modern Hebrew; 2) Classical Hebrew; 3) Hebrew and Semitic Linguistics.

IX. **Language - Other Jewish and Related Languages and Literatures**

> 1) Aramaic; 2) Yiddish; 3) Sephardic and Oriental Languages.

X. Literature

1) General; 2) Pre-Modern; 3) Modern Hebrew/Israeli; 4) Modern in other languages; 5) Jewish Literature in Translation.

XI. Near and Middle Eastern Studies

1) General Survey; 2) Pre-Modern Period; 3) Modern Period.

XII. Sephardic Studies

XIII. Social Sciences

1) General; 2) Local Jewish Communities; 3) Migration 4) Economy; 5) Politics.

XIV. State of Israel

1) History; 2) Society and Culture.

XV. Zionism

The index refers the reader to the general list of syllabi, which is arranged in alphabetical order.

I. ARCHAEOLOGY AND RELATED STUDIES

Cano Pérez   Universidad de Granada
Carter   University of Wisconsin
Gordon Harris
Greenspahn
Rubiato Díaz

II. ART

Baron   Schneebal
Garlick   Thompson
Nahir

III. BIBLE (See also: V.2; VII.2, 3; XI.1, 2)

1) Studies in the Hebrew Bible

Anderson D.	Keider
Boone	Kiley
Borg	Kraut
Brown J.	Lockshin
Brown M.	Mabee
Burnett	Mitchell
Cohn	Navarro Peiro
Combs	Olshen
Cooper	Orbach W.
Cutrer	Rabi
Eisenman	Robinson
Ensor	Shishido
Frerichs	Shively & Chapman
Frerichs & Mandelbaum	Steiglitz
Gittlen	Tullock
Good	Van Puffelen
Gordon Harris	Winkler
Greenspahn	University of Cape Town
Halpern	Universidad de Granada
Himmelfarb	University of Natal
Hughes	Oregon State University
Jensen	Rhodes University
Joiner	Wabash College
Johnson	West Virginia Wesleyan College

III. BIBLE (continued)

2) History of the Biblical Text

Carlton	Gordon Harris
Eisenmann	Greenspahn

3) Bible as Literature (See also X.2)

Albertson	Himmelfarb
Bogard	Kelly
Chively	Parvin
Cohn	Pérez Castro
Forrester	Reeves
Franco	Tigay
Frerichs & Hirsch	Torres Fernández
Garrison	Vaugham
Gary	Werner
Gordon Harris	University of Natal

IV. CONTEMPORARY JEWRY

(See also V.4, 5; VI; VII.5, 8, 9; X.3, 4, 5; XI; XIII; XIV)

Aranov	Katz M.
Auerbach	Katz S.
Avni	Keidar
Bankier	Neusner
Ben Rafael	Neusner & Flesher
Bok	Newman A.
Brown M.	Newman L.
Dash Moore	Ravven
Dashefsky	Rockaway
Encel	Sarason
Glazer	Schoenfeld
Heilman	Shimoni
Hyman A.	Verbit
Hyman P.	Weiner
Jaffee	Zuckerman A.
Katz I.	University of Washington at Seattle

V. HISTORY

1) General Survey

Ankori
Bankier
Blumberg
Chazan
Eisenman
Garber
Greenberg S.
Jospe
Oppenheim
Porter
Ravven

Signer
Sorenson
Stern M.
Twiss
Twiss & Sarason
Weill
Weiss
Universidad de Chile
Universidad de Granada
Prahran College of Advanced Education

2) Ancient History (See also I; III; VII.3; XI.2)

Aranov
Berdichevsky
Berner
Boone
Brown J.
Burstein
Cohn & Seeskin
Dean McBride
Eisenman
Ensor
Field
Finet
Good
Greenspahn
Hughes
Kraut
Lomasky
Macdonald

Maidman
McCready
Moehring
Myers & Spivack
Paltiel
Préaux
Rosenthal
Roth & Sacks
Rubiato Díaz
Stieglitz
Tigay
Trible
Universdad de Chile
Prahran College of Advanced Education
Universidade de São Paulo
University of Toronto
Wabash College

3) Medieval History (See also VII.4, 8; XI.2)

Ankori	Shatzmiller
Berner	Shenhar
Boid	Shmidman
Chazan	Stieglitz
Cohen M.	Stillman
Goodblatt	Universidad de Chile
Kraut	Universidad de Granada
Morony	Prahran College of Advanced Education
Nahon	Universidade de São Paulo
Robinson	University of Wisconsin
Serper	

4) Modern and Contemporary History

(See also IV; VI; VII.5; XI.3, 4; XIII; XIV; XV)

Auerbach	Maier
Avni	Minerbi
Bankier	Moscati
Berner	Mosse
Bok	Nahon
Brown M.	Newman A.
Cesarani	Sarna
Cohen M.	Sephiha
Dash Moore	Stein
Eliach	Steinberg
Encel	Stieglitz
Friesel	Stillman
Graebner	Weill
Herschkowitz	Weinberg
Hoffman	Weissbach
Hyman P.	Wertheimer
Katz S.	Zipperstein
Klecky	Zuckerman A.
Kochan	Universidad de Chile
Kornberg	Prahran College of Advanced Education
Kraut	Universidade de São Paulo
Landau	Victoria College
Lee M.	

V. HISTORY (continued)

5) Local History (See also XI; XIII.2; XIV.1)

Auerbach
Boehm
Bok
Brown M.
Challener & Weiss
Dash Moore
Davis, Rabb & Cohen
Feingold
Goldstein
Grumet
Gurock
Hershkowitz
Hyman P.
Kasson
Katz I.
Katz M.
Kochan
Landau
Lipstadt

McLoughlin
Moreno Koch
Nahon
Pinkus
Rabi
Ramer
Rischin
Sarna (2)
Shain
Stern M.
Stillman
Unger
Weill
Winer
Wertheimer
Zipperstein
University of Cincinnati
University of Toronto

6) Special Topics (See also VI; VII.8; XI; XV)

Ankori
Berner
Davies
Eisenman
Fenton
Glazer
Greenberg G.
Greenspahn
Hoffman
Horowitz
Kaplan
Kasson
Katz N.
Landau
Misrahi

Moehring
Nahon
Nussbaum
Paltiel
Rassekh
Rischin
Scherr
Stillman
Stillman & Sullivan
Twiss & Sarason
Williams W.
Zipperstein
Zúñiga
University of Toronto
University of Wisconsin

VI. HOLOCAUST STUDIES

1) History, Social and Religious Studies (See also V.4, 6)

Bankier	Marrus
Berger	Mason
Boozer & Blumenthal	Miller
Brown M.	Morley
Dobkowski	Oppenheim
Durnbaugh	Orbach A.
Eckardt	Orbach W.
Eliach	Porter
Fierman	Porton
Frizzell	Raphael, M.
Garber	Renn
Gershenzon	Ruether
Greenberg B	Ryan
Greenberg G.	Scholnik
Greenberg I.	Scult
Greenspahn	Sherwin
Kennet	Slavin
Knopp	Stadtler
Kornberg	Stein
Kraut	Thompson & Bonkowski
Lacocque & Manschreck	Tiefel
Lee M.	Woodworth
Lee & Steele	Zuckerman A.
Lipstadt	Zygielbaum
Littell & Knopp	McGill University

2) Literature (See also X.3, 4)

Alexander	Pelli
Angress	Pfefferkorn
Bier	Rose
Eliach	Rosenfeld
Fagin	Roskies
Felstiner	Sherwin
Langer	Zygielbaum
Norich	

VII.   JUDAISM AND JEWISH THOUGHT

1) General Survey

Ankori
Aranov & Puterman
Avery Peck
Barylko
Berger
Berner
Blementhal
Boid
Cano Pérez
Carlton
Cohn
Ellenson
Fasbender
Fenton
Gabriel
Garber
Garshowitz
Greenberg S.
Halperin
Himmelfarb
Kiener
Kogan
Kraus
Lary
Lee H.
Lockshin
Neusner
Neusner & Jaffee
Neusner, Peck & Gordon

Nussbaum
Oppenheim
Orbach W.
Paltiel
Planer
Porton
Puterman
Rosenberg
Rosenthal
Sarason
Seidler-Feller
Shmidman
Stern M.
Tanenzapf
Umansky
Vogel
Waller & Neuman
Weiss
Wylen
University of Cape Town
Universidad de Chile
Universidad de Granada
McGill University
University of Natal
Prahran College of Advanced Education
University of Regina
Purdue University
Universidade de São Paulo

2) Religion (See also III; VII.8)

Albertson
Aranov
Askenazi
Brooks
Brown J.
Cannon
Cooper
Dash Moore
Dietrich
Eisenman
Eslinger
Frerichs
Garber
Good
Greenberg S.
Greenspahn
Gurock
Halperin D.
Halpern
Heilman
Himmelfarb
Hosoi
Hyman A.
Jaffee
Joiner
Kraut
Lee H.
Liebman

Lomasky
Lowenstein
McReady
Moehring
Neusner
Orr
Patterson & Vogel
Porter
Porton
Ravven
Reeder
Reeder & Jaffee
Reynolds
Sanders
Sarason
Shishido
Shmidman
Steuer
Stites
Tanenzapf
Tiefel
Twiss
Twiss & Frerichs
Vogel
Williams P.
Yonker
Zaidman
University of Cape Town

3) Ancient Judaism (See also III; V.2; XI.2)

Aranov
Avery Peck
Boone
Carlton
Cooper
Eslinger
Feldman
Fox
Halpern
Himmelfarb

Kraut
Lee H.
Mendelson
Moehring
Neusner
Raphael F.
Roth & Sacks
Tigay
University of Notre Dame
Wabash College

116

4) Rabbinic and Medieval Judaism (See also V.3)

Ankori
Barth
Bowman
Falk
Fox
Garber
Garshowitz
Goodblatt
Greenspahn
Halperin D.
Halperin & Newby

Himmelfarb
Hyman A.
Jospe
Kraut
Lasker
Lockshin
Neusner
Newman L.
Robinson
Rose
Shmidman

5) Modern and Contemporary Judaism

(See also IV; V.4; X.3, 4, 5; XIII; XIV.2; XV)

Aranov
Avery Peck
Blumenthal
Bok
Dash Moore
Dietrich
Eisen
Eisenman
Heilman
Horowitz
Hyman A.
Jospe
Katz N.
Katz S.
Landau
Moscati

Nahon
Newman
Orbach A.
Orbach W.
Raphael M.
Ravven
Rippin
Robinson
Sarason
Schoenfeld
Shimoni
Umansky
Vogel
Weissler
Wertheimer
Prahran College of Advanced Education

6) Mysticism

Berger
Blumenthal
Jaffee
Jospe

Rose
Talmage
Weiss

7) Ethics

Ellenson
Hyman A.
Reeder
Reeder & Sarason
Stern M.

Tanenzapf
Twiss
Twiss & Little
Umansky
Weiss

8) Judaism and Christianity (See also III; VI)

Ankori
Aranov
Beck
Berger
Berner
Dietrich
Frerichs
Garshowitz
Gero
Greenberg B.
Halperin
Kraut
Littell & Knopp

Lomasky
McCready
Minerbi
Moehring
Nahon
Porton
Reynolds
Rose
Ruether
Ryan
Van Buren
Vogel

VII. JUDAISM AND JEWISH THOUGHT (continued)

9) Other Special Topics (See also III; IV; VI; XI; XIV; XV)

Askenazi
Avery Peck
Baumgarten
Cohn
Collings
Cutter
Diament
Eisen
Good
Greenberg G.
Greenberg S.
Grumet
Gurock
Halperin D.
Hanni
Herman
Hyman A.
Jaffee
Jospe
Kasson
Katz N.
Kraut
Lacocque & Manschreck
Lasker
Liebman
Nelson

Neusner
Neusner & Flesher
Neusner, Peck & Gordon
Newman L.
Passamaneck
Passelecq
Porter
Porton
Raphael F.
Ravven
Rose
Rosenthal
Sarason
Scherr
Sojcher
Stern S.
Stites
Szafran
Turniansky
Umansky
Vogel
Vorspan
Weissler
Wertheimer
Prahran College of Advanced Education

1) General and Modern Hebrew

Anderson J.	Nahir
Avery Peck	Navarro Peiro
Braun	Penacchietti & Trevisan
Cano Pérez	Sabar
Devens	Sáenz Badillos
Dori	Vegas Montaner
Fales	Wasserman
Felkin	University of Cape Town
Girón Blanc	Universidad de Chile
Gordon Harris	Universidad de Granada
Kronfeld	Los Angeles Valley College
Macdonald	Universidade de São Paulo
Morahg	University of Toronto
Moraldi	University of Wisconsin

2) Classical Hebrew

Brooks	Pérez Castro
Craigie	Sabar
Morahg	Sarason
Newman L.	Strus
Peck	

3) Hebrew and Semitic Linguistics

Fales	Sabar
Gordon	Sánchez
Moraldi	Zúñiga
Rosen	Universidad de Granada

120

IX. LANGUAGE – OTHER JEWISH AND RELATED LANGUAGES AND LITERATURE

(See also X.1, 4)

1) Aramaic

Fernández Vallina
Peral Torres

Torres Fernández
University of Wisconsin

2) Yiddish

Derczansky
Kronfeld
Roskies
Walden

Zuckerman M.
Zygielbaum
Prahran College of Advanced Education

3) Sephardic and Oriental Languages

Sephiha (3)

Universidad de Granada

X. LITERATURE

1) General (See also IX.2, 3)

Carlton
Morahg
Moscati
Pennacchietti & Trevisan
Schoville
Sephiha

Sirat
Tanenzapf
Taylor
Tigay
University of Natal
Universidade de São Paulo

X. LITERATURE (continued)

2) Pre-Modern (See also III.3)

Albertson
Barth
Bogard
Cohn
Cooper
Garber
Garrison
Garshowitz
Girón Blanc
Jospe
Kreiman
Navarro Piero
Newman L.
Parvin

Pérez Castro
Rose
Rosenthal
Sáenz Badillos
Sarason
Torres Fernández
Vaugham
Zygielbaum
Universidad de Chile
Universidad de Granada
University of Natal
Universidade de São Paulo
University of Wisconsin
York University

3) Modern Hebrew/Israeli Literature (See also VI.2)

Avery Peck
Devens
Felkin
Kronfeld
Mazor
Morahg

Patterson & Vogel
Pelli
Sáenz Badillos
Zahavy
Universidade de São Paulo
University of Wisconsin

4) Modern Literature in Other Languages (See also VI.2; IX.2, 3)

Auster
Berger
Bier
Halperin I.
Jaffee
Kronfeld
Nadell

Novak
Roskies
Shapiro
Spatz
Walden
Zuckerman M.
Prahran College of Advanced Education

X. LITERATURE (continued)

5) Jewish Literature in Translation

Frerichs & Mandelbaum	Lasker
Garber	Morahg
Jospe	Zuckerman M.
Kronfeld	University of California - Los Angeles

XI. NEAR AND MIDDLE EASTERN STUDIES

1) General Survey

Ankori	Rassekh
Harris	Stern M.

2) Pre-Modern Period

Berdichevsky	Hughes
Burstein	Macdonald
Finet	Maidman
Good	Morony
Halpern	Sanders

3) Modern Period

Israeli	Rassekh
Kennet	Stillman

XII. SEPHARDIC STUDIES

(See also V.5, 6; VII.9; XI; IX.3)

Ankori	Stern M.
Goldberg	Stillman
Kaplan	Universidad de Granada
Moreno Koch	University of Toronto
Nahon	University of Wisconsin
Sephiha	

XIII. SOCIAL SCIENCES

1) General

Ablin and Avivi
Aranov
Ben Rafael
Bensimon
Bok
Cano Pérez
Davids
Derczansky
Encel
Herman
Hodara
Katz N.

Keidar
Lipstadt
Littell & Knopp
Mehlman
Nahon
Porter
Robinson
Rose
Schoenfeld
Seidler-Feller
Zuckerman A.

2) Local Jewish Communities (See also XIV.2)

Blasi
Brown M.
Cohen S.
Dash Moore
Dashefsky
Glazer
Goldstein
Heilman
Himmelfarb
Hyman P.
Jick
Jospe
Kasson
Katz M.

Kranzler
Nadell
Pinkus
Porter
Rabi
Rischin
Verbit
Waller
Weinfeld
Wertheimer
Williams P.
Zenner
Prahran College of Advanced Education

3) Migrations

Avni	Rischin
Bok	

4) Economy

Don	Helman

5) Politics

Waller	Zuckerman A.

XIV. STATE OF ISRAEL

(See also V.4)

1) History

Auerbach	Kochan
Ben Ami	Ruether
Delmaire	University of Cincinnati
Garber	Universidad de Granada

2) Society and Culture

Ben Rafael	Helman
Blasi	Liebman
Don	Near
Goldstein	University of Cincinnati

XV. ZIONISM

(See also IV; V.4; VI; XI.3, 4)

Bowman
Eisenman
Garber
Goodblatt
Greenberg S.
Lipstadt

Liwerant
Neusner
Newman L.
Raphael M.
Sarason
Umansky

PART THREE

Patterns in the University Teaching of Jewish History

PATTERNS IN THE UNIVERSITY TEACHING OF JEWISH HISTORY

Mervin F. Verbit

The only global collection of data on the teaching of Jewish
Civilization in institutions of higher learning is now housed at the
International Center for University Teaching of Jewish Civilization in
Jerusalem. Although the collection is not complete or systematic in
the technical-statistical sense of the term, it is, nevertheless, large
enough to provide an empirical basis for going beyond impressionistic
analysis alone in understanding how Jewish Civilization is taught at
the university level. The present paper is a brief analysis of the
material available at the Center on one subject in the field of Jewish
Civilization, namely, Jewish history.

As of the end of 1984, the Center's files included 1,042 courses in
Jewish history, and these courses constitute the data on which this
paper is based. Syllabi are available for 133 of the courses, formal
descriptions are available for 358, and the remaining 551 are listed by
title alone. Regarding the age of the data, 387 of the courses were
offered in 1983 and/or 1984, 406 were offered in 1980-82, and 174
courses are dated 1975-79, although there is every reason to believe
that they remained in the curriculum after that date. (No dates are
available for the remaining 75 courses.)

Of the 1,042 courses, 792 are from institutions in the United
States, 92 are from Canada, 20 are from Latin America, 122 are from
Europe (mostly England), and 16 are from other parts of the world.
Seven hundred and seventy-four are offered in universities, 144 are in

127

four-year liberal arts colleges, 20 are in community colleges, teachers colleges, or other specialized schools, 40 are given in church-related institutions (all in the United States), and the remaining 64 courses are taught in institutions whose character is not identified in the records of the Center. Of the 605 courses for which the information is available, 22 per cent are year-long courses, 77 per cent are semester or trimester courses, and one per cent are shorter units. Of the 341 courses for which the number of academic credits is specified, two-thirds (66 per cent) carry three credits, 12 per cent carry four credits, 11 per cent are shorter (one or two credits), and 11 per cent are longer (five or more credits).

While there is no way to know whether these 1,042 courses are precisely representative of all Jewish history courses offered in institutions of higher learning, it is reasonable to assume that they are not significantly skewed in their character. Some countries and some areas within countries were covered more thoroughly than others by the Center's collection of material. However, there is not likely to be what social scientists call "selective bias" to any significant extent with regard to such characteristics of the courses as their departmental contexts, their prerequisites, or their content.

Jewish history can be taught in any one of several conventional academic departments. Sometimes the decision about where to house a course is made on intellectual and conceptual grounds. Perhaps even more often it is made on the basis of available faculty and willing colleagues. Even where there is a Department of Jewish (or Judaic) Studies, Jewish history courses need not all be housed in that department. Indeed, we know that in some institutions that have such a department, courses in Jewish history are sometimes found in the history and sociology departments as well as in the Department of Judaic Studies. The advantages and disadvantages of the various kinds of academic "homes" for courses in Jewish Civilization are an important matter because the context of teaching necessarily influences what is taught.

We find that, of the 957 courses for which information is available about their departmental homes (Table 1), 32 per cent are taught in departments of Jewish Studies, 22 per cent are in history departments, and 35 per cent are in religion departments. The remaining 11 per cent are in humanities (5 per cent), social science (2 per cent), Oriental Studies (2 per cent), and Middle or Near Eastern Studies (2 per cent). The Jewish history courses in Europe are more likely to be found in Jewish Studies or Oriental Studies departments (51 and 29 per cent, respectively). North American courses are more often located in religion departments than in any other single department.

It thus seems that North American universities are likely to view Jewish history less often as part of general history than as a component of religious studies. To what extent that fact is antecedent to the departmental location of Jewish history courses and to what extent it is a consequence of other factors which lead to Jewish history being taught by members of religion departments needs further investigation. Still, the fact itself is likely to have implications for the way that students view the Jewish experience and the way in which the courses are designed.

It is often hard to know the specific content of a course from its title or official description. Sometimes even the syllabus leaves several important questions about content unanswered. On one such

129

question, namely, whether Jewish thought is explicitly included, information was available for about one-half (518) of the courses. There was explicit mention of Jewish thought in the descriptions, syllabi, or titles of 60 per cent of those courses, with some variation by the department in which a course is given. Jewish Studies departments are most likely explicitly to include Jewish thought (65 per cent). Religion and general humanities departments are somewhat less likely (61 and 60 per cent, respectively). Fifty-nine per cent of the courses in history departments explicitly mention Jewish thought. Half of the twelve courses in social science departments for which information is available include explicit mention of Jewish thought, as do 64 per cent of the eleven courses in Middle Eastern Studies departments. While the data are such that not too much should be made of these comparisons, it is worth noting that more often than not the Jewish experience is presented not only as what the Jews did, but also as how they interpreted what they did.

Prerequisites for courses reflect two decisions made by universities about those courses. One concerns the level at which courses are taught, since advanced courses require students to have acquired some prior substantive or disciplinary background. The second can suggest a way in which some institutions discourage enrollment in selected courses by imposing more prerequisites than the material itself demands or than are required for comparable courses.

Information about prerequisites is available for 499 of the courses in the collection analyzed in this report. Of those courses, 76 per cent require no previous university study, and the prerequisites that are given for the other courses (24 per cent) show no particular pattern. The three departments in which Jewish history courses are most

130

often given (Jewish Studies, religion and history) do not differ in their likelihood to impose prerequisites; 23, 26, and 22 per cent of the courses in those departments, respectively, have such requirements. Courses in general humanities and social science departments are less likely to have prerequisites, but in both cases the samples are small. Jewish history courses in Oriental Studies departments are most likely to have prerequisites (59 per cent), but here, too, the sample is small.

Jewish history covers several periods spread over four millenia and can, of course, be organized in many different ways. In this regard, the courses in our sample show some interesting patterns. (As has already been observed, the courses are not necessarily a technically representative sample, but they are probably not too atypical.)

Seventeen per cent of the courses are general surveys of Jewish history, with the remaining 83 per cent covering some defined part of the historic Jewish experience. Twenty-six per cent of the courses are in the Biblical period alone, and another six per cent cover a longer span including the Biblical period. If the survey courses are included (and allowing for rounding), 48 per cent of all the courses in Jewish history somehow include the Biblical period. Courses in post-Biblical Jewish history up to modern times are less frequent. Excluding the general survey courses, two per cent of the courses deal exclusively with the Second Temple period and an additional eight per cent include that period in the framework of a larger course. The comparable figures for the other periods are: Rabbinic, 2 and 7; Gaonic, less than 1 and 5; Medieval, 4 and 10.

The Modern and Contemporary periods are harder to analyze neatly because they frequently overlap in courses and because they include several topics around which separate courses are often given (e.g., Holocaust, Zionism, Israel). The 1,042 courses on which this report is based include the following:

Modern Jewish History (no explicit mention of Contemporary Period) 91
Contemporary Jewry   45
Modern and Contemporary Jewish History   110
Holocaust   71
Zionism and Israel   40

In other words, a total of 357 (or 34 per cent) of the more limited courses touch in one way or another on the Modern and Contemporary periods, or 51 per cent if we include the general survey courses.

These figures lead to several observations. The first is that there are fewer general survey courses that might have been expected. While that fact suggests a degree of focus and depth that is welcome, it also means that the total sweep of Jewish history is not presented in a single course as often as might be desirable.

It is also clear that the periods more often covered in university courses in Jewish history are the Biblical period and the Modern-Contemporary era. Approximately one-third of the courses (not counting the general surveys) covers each of these periods. Twenty-three per cent of the courses touch on the over two millenia between the Biblical and the modern eras, with emphasis in decreasing order on the Medieval, the Second Temple, the Rabbinic and the Gaonic periods.

As would be expected, the church-related institutions place more emphasis on the Biblical period than do other schools. While 30 per cent of the courses cover the Biblical period (not counting general surveys) in "secular" institutions, 55 per cent of the courses in church-related schools do so. The fact remains, however, that the 30 per cent in non-church institutions is a significantly high figure, and fully a quarter of the Jewish history courses in those institutions deal with the Biblical period alone.

It is also interesting that only seven per cent of the courses are on the Holocaust. It is widely believed that one of the imbalances in the teaching of Jewish history in universities is an over-emphasis on the Holocaust. Indeed, many commentators have expressed concern that many students' only knowledge of Jewish history will be about the Holocaust. It may well be that far more students learn about the Holocaust than about the rest of the Jewish experience because, without figures on enrollment, we do not know how many students take which courses. However, our data clearly suggest that if students do study only the Holocaust period, it is not for lack of opportunity to explore the other eras in Jewish history.

The balance among offerings in the various periods of Jewish history is not uniform. There are comparatively fewer general survey courses in Europe and Canada than in the U.S. (13, 14, and 19 per cent, respectively) and relatively fewer courses in the Biblical period in the U.S. (26 per cent, as compared with 32 per cent for Canada and 34 per cent for Europe). The "Middle" era--including the Second Temple, Rabbinic, Gaonic and Medieval periods--is proportionately more often covered in Europe and Canada (34 per cent and 30 per cent of the courses, respectively) than in the U.S. (21 per cent). The Modern-

Contemporary period is covered most often in Europe (43 per cent of the courses) and least often in Canada (32 per cent), with the U.S. between the two (39 per cent). The courses in other parts of the world in the material used for this report are too few in number to justify statistical analysis. (It should be noted that here, as elsewhere in this paper, the percentages occasionally total more than one hundred. That is so because several courses which are not general surveys still cover more than one of the major periods of history and thus count more than once.)

The balance of offerings varies not only by country, but also by the extent of other courses in Jewish history and in Hebrew available at the same institution. The relationship is sharpest and most consistent with the number of Jewish history courses taught. As seen in Table 2, the larger the number of Jewish history courses offered in an institution, the smaller the proportion of those courses that are general surveys or that deal with the Biblical period and the larger the proportion that concern the "Middle" and Modern-Contemporary periods; the differences are considerable.

The relationship with the level of Hebrew offered is not quite so consistent (Table 3). In general, the more advanced the level of Hebrew taught at an institution, the larger is the proportion of Jewish history courses dealing with the "Middle" and the Modern-Contemporary periods and the smaller the proportion of courses covering the Biblical period. However, a relatively large proportion of the Jewish history courses in institutions with no Hebrew language program at all deals with the Modern-Contemporary period. Also, those institutions which offer only elementary Hebrew have almost two-thirds of their courses in Jewish history focused on the Biblical period, and, while courses in church-related schools are overrepresented in this group, their weight comes nowhere near accounting for this heavy emphasis on the Biblical period.

As we might expect, there is a relationship between the level of Hebrew taught in an institution and the number of Jewish history courses in its curriculum. The relationship is positive and consistent, but it becomes dramatic only at the upper level.

The balance among the different periods varies not only by institutional type, but also by department, as seen in Table 4. Humanities and Middle Eastern Studies departments show the most even balance among the periods of Jewish history in their offerings. Oriental Studies departments also have a substantial proportion of their courses in each of the major periods, although with some emphasis on the Biblical period. Departments of Jewish Studies place increasing emphasis on the later periods, as do history departments. Religion departments heavily emphasize the Biblical period, and social science departments concentrate almost totally, as would be expected, on the Modern-Contemporary period. The differences among departments with regard to the likelihood of their offering general survey courses are not especially large, except that Oriental Studies departments offer relatively few such courses.

As expected, the general survey courses are least likely to have prerequisites (nine per cent). The more specific courses do not vary significantly by period regarding the likelihood of their requiring prior background. Twenty-eight per cent of the courses covering the Biblical and the "Middle" periods and 25 per cent of courses dealing with the Modern-Contemporary period have prerequisites.

135

The courses in the Biblical period are much less likely to include explicit mention of Jewish Thought in their official descriptions (29 per cent) than are courses in the "Middle" (62 per cent) and the Modern-Contemporary (72 per cent) periods. General surveys are the most likely to mention the inclusion of Jewish thought (76 per cent). It may be that courses in the history of the Biblical period are more limited because they are seen as supplementary to courses in the Bible itself, while courses in the other periods are designed to include both Jewish life and thought within a single framework.

Probably for the same reason, the courses in the Biblical period are shorter, carrying an average of 3.1 credits. General surveys and courses covering the "Middle" period both average 3.2 credits, and the Modern-Contemporary courses carry an average of 3.4 credits.

The foregoing analysis has two important limitations. The 1,042 courses on which it is based were not, as noted above, collected in a way that can be claimed to provide a representative sample. However, there were no systematic biases in the way in which the material was gathered. As a result, while there is likely to be some statistical error, the figures reported here are probably not too far from suggesting the actual characteristics of all Jewish history courses now included in university curricula. Secondly, the analysis is only quantitative. No attempt is made here to assess the many qualitative issues that deserve attention. To do so would require the development of criteria and their application in ways that are not possible on the basis of official descriptions and syllabi alone. Nevertheless, even the quantitative data provide at least the outlines of a very interesting picture worth further reflection.

Table 1. Departmental Context of Courses in Jewish History, by Region
        (Percentages)

		Region				
	Total	U.S.	Canada	Europe	Latin America	Other
Department						
Jewish (Judaic) Studies	32	29	30	51	60	62
History	22	24	18	8	0	31
Religion	35	39	37	8	0	0
Humanities	5	4	8	4	40	0
Social Sciences	2	3	1	0	0	0
Middle (Near) Eastern Studies	2	1	5	1	0	6
Oriental Studies	2	0	0	29	0	0
Total	100	100	99	101	100	99
N	957	752	92	77	20	16

(Note: Because of rounding, percentages do not always add up to 100.)

137

Table 2. Periods of Jewish History Covered in Courses, by the Number
          of Jewish History Courses in the Institution's Curriculum
          (Percentages)

Period	Number of Jewish History Courses			
	1-3	4-6	7-13	14 or more
General Survey	29	17	15	7
Biblical Period	38	29	21	15
Biblical and "Middle" Periods	3	1	1	1
"Middle" Period	7	19	21	21
"Middle" and Modern-Contemporary Periods	3	2	4	14
Modern-Contemporary Period	21	32	38	42
Total	101	100	100	100
N	258	251	271	241

Table 3. Periods of Jewish History Covered in Courses, by the Level
of Hebrew Offered in the Institution (Percentages)

	Level of Hebrew				
	None	Elementary	Intermediate	Advanced	Literature
Period					
General Survey	24	18	22	23	9
Biblical Period	30	59	30	23	17
Biblical and "Middle" Periods	0	5	1	2	2
"Middle" Period	9	8	16	15	23
"Middle" and Modern-Contemporary Periods	1	0	3	6	9
Modern-Contemporary Period	37	10	29	31	40
Total	101	100	101	100	100
N	104	39	160	108	443

Table 4. Periods of Jewish History Covered in Courses, by Department
            (Percentages)

	Department						
Period	Jewish Studies	History	Religion	Humanities	Social Sciences	Middle Eastern Studies	Oriental Studies
General Survey	16	18	21	12	14	20	5
Biblical Period	17	10	45	28	5	33	32
Biblical and "Middle" Periods	1	1	1	0	0	0	14
"Middle" Period	22	18	14	22	0	13	13
"Middle" and Modern-Contemporary Periods	7	5	1	12	0	13	0
Modern-Contemporary Period	38	47	18	26	82	20	36
Total	101	99	100	100	101	99	100
N	301	201	329	50	22	15	22

INSTITUTIONS OF HIGHER LEARNING THAT TEACH JEWISH CIVILIZATION

The World Register's source material for each institution is indicated by the following codes:

B   The institution publishes a brochure, available in the World Register, about its offerings in Jewish Civilization

Bm   The institution publishes a substantive magazine in Jewish Civilization. Copy is in the World Register

D   The institution has a separate Department of Judaic (or Jewish) Studies

F   The names of instructors of courses in Jewish Civilization are listed in the World Register

G   Information about graduate courses in Jewish Civilization is in the World Register

P   The institution has a special program in Jewish Civilization

Sc   The World Register has a complete collection of the institution's syllabi or course descriptions in Jewish Civilization

Sp   The World Register has a partial collection of the institution's syllabi or course descriptions in Jewish Civilization

Tc   The World Register has a complete collection of the institution's course titles in Jewish Civilization

Tp   The World Register has a partial collection of the institution's course titles in Jewish Civilization